Studymates

Many other titles in preparation

Writing Your Master's Thesis

Edited by Alan Bond

www.**studymates**.co.uk

© 2004 Alan Bond, John Brierley, Allison Coleman, Mark Goodwin, Norma Green, Chris Harding, Karen Mortimer, Gina Preston, Mark Tippett, John Williams, Colin Wight

First published in 2004 by Studymates Limited, PO Box 2, Bishops Lydeard, Somerset TA3 3YE, United Kingdom

Telephone: (01823) 432002
Fax: (01823) 430097

Typeset by PDQ Typesetting, Newcastle-under-Lyme
Printed and bound in Great Britain

Contents

List of Illustrations

Figures

Tables

Preface

The original impetus for the book came from the fact that, whilst director of an MSc programme by distance-learning at the University of Wales Aberystwyth, it was clear that there was a very real problem in communicating to students, based at a distance, just what might be expected in a Master's dissertation. In fact, it also seemed to be the case that for full-time Master's students, there was an often unwarranted assumption (on behalf of the academics involved) that the knowledge of what was expected and how tasks might be undertaken was greater than it should have been. Initial attempts to address the problem for the distance-learning students led to the development of a 'thesis school' which students attended before starting their Master's research. Feedback from the school was excellent, and publishing the same sort of advice handed out at that school seemed too great an opportunity to miss.

Early planning of the book, then, revolved around all the questions Master's students might ask at stages before embarking on their research, until after they had submitted. Selecting appropriate members of staff to cover the diversity of advice needed was actually very easy in a university environment and I had been fortunate to have many colleagues give up their time for free, often at weekends, to provide input to the 'thesis school'. However, it was then that the first mistake was made (and I hope the co-authors will forgive this bit)! To increase credibility, authors selected were invariably at the top of their field, but these are very busy people and getting copy from them, bearing in mind the already oversubscribed nature of their diaries, proved difficult. So, whilst some authors laboured, others had to wait. Editing some chapters also ruffled feathers because I have many years of experience of producing distance-learning materials where readability is all important and split infinitives and other grammatical horrors are more-or-less ignored in such a context (or even embraced in their place).

Through all this, as each chapter finally surfaced, my belief that this guide would be useful to all those who read it has made it worth the wait. I'm very happy with the result and am very grateful to all the authors for putting up with all the delays and my assassination of their writing style.

To you, the reader, I make this promise. I have assembled a truly professional team, and they have delivered what is, in my judgment, superb advice for any student. Read what they have to say, listen to their voices, learn from their experiences and you too will achieve your goal of writing your Master's Thesis.

Between them, the authors have experience of working in many universities, although when the project started, all the authors were at the same one. I believe that this wealth of experience of different university environments means that this book provides advice which is universally applicable.

Alan Bond (Editor)

1

Planning and Organising a Master's Thesis
Chris Harding

One-minute summary – This chapter will consider the objectives and scope of a Master's thesis and the process of designing and organising the research necessary to produce such a thesis. It will also examine the supervisory relationship, so as to indicate the level of assistance and guidance which may be expected from a supervisor.

The following main issues will be discussed:

▶ introducing the objectives in completing a Master's thesis
▶ choosing the subject for research
▶ planning and managing your time
▶ designing your research
▶ working with your supervisor.

Introducing the objectives in completing a Master's thesis

Writing a thesis is an exercise in carrying out research and writing an account of that research activity. If you have not completed a research dissertation as part of your undergraduate course this may be your first experience of a sustained research exercise. Since a Master's thesis is part of a postgraduate scheme of study, more will be expected of you compared to the kind of assignment you would usually have been given as an undergraduate.

Firstly, the scale of the activity is likely to be much larger. Typically, work on a Master's thesis will comprise about one third of the time and effort within your degree scheme (usually a period of three or four months' work after the taught part of the programme has been completed). If your university uses a credit system, it is likely that 60 credits will be assigned to the thesis component of the degree out of a total of 180 credits for one year of postgraduate study. Most degree regulations will usually specify that the thesis should be between 15,000 and 20,000 words in length. All of this should provide you with some idea of the amount of work involved in the thesis. To put this into context, if you double space your work, you should probably expect to produce about 50 pages of work depending on the nature of the research and the number of diagrams, if any.

Secondly, there is a qualitative difference between a Master's thesis and a typical undergraduate essay. As an undergraduate, the titles and subjects of your written work will usually have been set for you. As a postgraduate, you will be

1

expected to select an appropriate topic for research yourself, which will then be approved by your supervisor and department. You will be also be expected to probe the subject further and use more sophisticated research methodology. In short, your role will be much more independent.

It may be helpful to locate the Master's thesis within an educational context. On the one hand, it will involve a more substantial exercise in research and academic writing compared to your undergraduate experience. On the other hand, less will be expected of you, as regards both the scale and level of the work, compared to the requirements of a full postgraduate research degree (either MPhil or PhD). Viewed in this way, the Master's thesis provides a bridge between the 'taught' element in higher education and study through independent research activity. You can thus see your work on the thesis as a short period of apprenticeship in research activity, or the first stage in developing crucial generic research skills, in particular those of identifying a worthwhile research topic, planning research and organising time, locating and using research data and organising and writing an account of the research.

Choosing the subject for research

As this is an exercise in independent research, your first task will be to identify an appropriate subject to be covered in a Master's thesis. To be able to do this you will need to be familiar with your wider field of study and you will need an ability to identify, from your earlier study of the subject, interesting and significant questions which merit further enquiry or discussion. For many students, especially those just embarking on research activity, this may be one of the most difficult parts of the whole exercise. What is worthwhile in research terms is unlikely to be as obvious to the relative novice as to the seasoned academic researcher. This is not something to worry about, however, as the supervisor's role is to provide just this sort of advice.

You may well already have developed ideas about possible research topics during the earlier part of your course: seminar discussions or written assignments may have raised unresolved points of interest and triggered the suggestion of further enquiry. For example, a science student may have discussed the perception that an oil spill has brought a particular species of sea bird close to extinction. As this was a perception, and there were no actual facts to back this up, you might decide that it was a worthy topic for investigation. Remember that, however, while the choice of subject for research should be essentially your decision, you will be expected to take the opportunity to discuss possibilities with your supervisor, and perhaps other staff if appropriate, and in any case you will not be allowed to proceed with a project which is academically worthless or unworkable. Thus your choice of subject will be made subject to guidance and advice. Taking the same example, it may be that you discuss this idea with your supervisor, who then refers you to research published recently which answers the

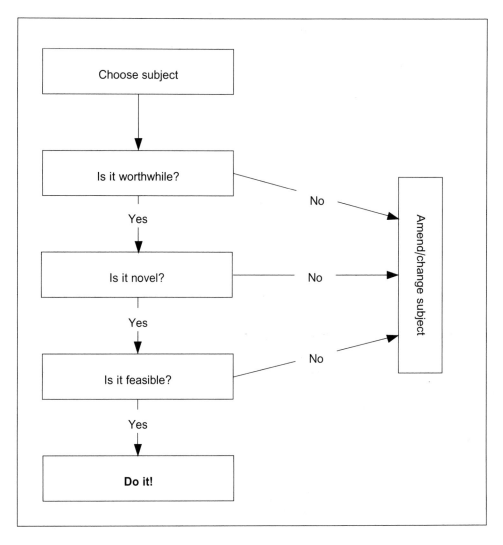

Figure 1. Choosing your subject.

questions you were hoping to investigate in your thesis. Whilst disappointing, this discussion has saved you a lot of time!

There are both academic and practical considerations you should bear in mind when choosing the subject for research. In academic terms, the subject should comprise problems of significance and/or a topic which has not received very much attention as yet so that there are genuine questions which have not been fully or satisfactorily answered or material which has not been extensively studied. You may be advised, for instance, that a subject 'has been done to death' or that 'this is a well-trodden path', implying that there is little which would be new to say about the subject, and that it would not therefore be appropriate to write your thesis on it.

In practical terms there will necessarily be limits as regards what you will be able to achieve within a period of a few months. An awareness of the time and resources actually at your disposal should constrain your choice of subject and, remember, it is a good idea to ask your supervisor at an early stage for an opinion on your research plan to get an early warning about over-ambitious plans which cannot be completed within the deadline.

Your choice of subject should therefore be informed by a number of basic questions which are illustrated in Figure 1 and explained in more detail below.

► Does the subject raise genuine and interesting questions? (Is it worthwhile?)
► To what extent has the ground been covered by other researchers? (Is it novel?)
► Can the subject be adequately covered, in terms of being researched and written up, in the time available ? (Is it feasible?)

The other important point to bear in mind is that there is limited time available for making this initial, though crucial, decision. In practice, some Master's students are able to give the question some thought at an earlier point in the course, for instance when ideas first occur to them, by discussing the suitability and potential of the subject with academic staff in advance of the date for properly starting work on the thesis. It may well be an advantage, then, to give the matter some preliminary thought earlier on. In any event, avoid getting bogged down in choosing a topic at the beginning of the research period. Although good supervisors will be alert to this danger, you cannot rely on a supervisor continually to chase you to get started.

Planning and managing your time

In any programme of research, an appreciation of the timescale of the project is essential. In the case of a thesis, the timescale is defined for you by the starting and submission dates (for instance, June – when the taught part of the programme is complete – and the end of September – for submission). It is worth noting that some universities' regulations allow a longer period before the submission deadline, but a timescale of three months is widely recognised as being adequate and, unless there are good reasons, potential employers may question why it has taken longer. Having fixed dates at least provides you with a frame for a timetable and you should then consider (again, often this will be in consultation with the supervisor) how much of the time available you should allocate to the key phases of your research and writing up. Much will of course depend upon the more precise subject of the research and such matters as the availability of materials and the method being used to collect data.

Remember that there are two main types of activity involved in the production of any kind of thesis: the research and the writing up. You certainly need to consider the proportion of available time necessary for each of these key tasks and take care at the earlier stage not to be over-optimistic about the speed at which you can write up the results of your research in an organised and lucid form. Writing up often takes longer than most researchers wish or expect, especially the technical aspects of the process, such as referencing and producing tables, diagrams or other special types of format.

Ideally you should have a clear and realistic timetable, checked and approved by your supervisor, worked out as soon as possible. This can then help to give you some sense of where you are going and at what speed.

Designing your research

In some ways, the conventional format of a research thesis in itself supplies a structure within which to define your research effort. A glance at a number of completed theses will reveal that they are usually laid out in a series of more or less uniform stages: an introductory section which explains the scope, objectives and methods of the research, and provides some background information and a statement on existing literature on the subject by way of supplying context; a main section reporting on the research; and a concluding section summarising and discussing the research outcomes. You may sometimes feel constrained by the conventions of the thesis style and presentation, but these conventions do in effect tell you how to lay out the thesis in broad terms. Obviously, rules or recommendations about the length of the thesis will immediately determine the size and scope of the research. But also bear in mind that the production of a thesis is a self-contained research exercise with an educational point – to prove and judge your ability in carrying out and writing about research. Therefore, you will be expected to produce the thesis in a certain form.

The research exercise is called a thesis for a particular reason. 'Thesis' means 'argument' and it is expected that you will not just carry out research in the sense of uncovering a subject (what you might call the 'spadework') but that you will also demonstrate that there is point in what you are doing – that it has some value in terms of improving knowledge and understanding of the subject. This process of showing the academic worth of your work will in practice comprise the argument of your thesis. It is always useful to remember the distinction between good academic work, which should have some value for society, and more personally motivated research which is usually described as a 'hobby'. Most people have personal interests which may be fascinating for them as individuals, but not necessarily of significance or value for others. It is part of the rigour of academic research that it requires a justification over and above mere personal interest, and one of the elements of the argument you should present in your thesis is the reason why your chosen topic and line of enquiry is of wider value.

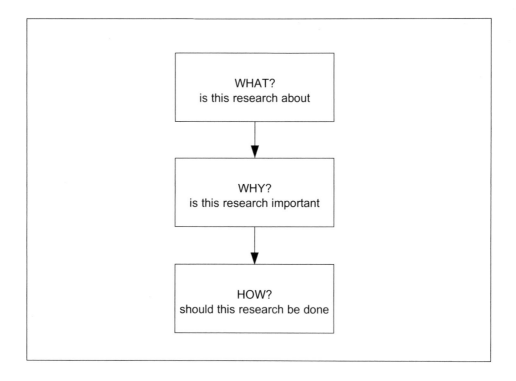

Figure 2. Designing your research.

This process of demonstrating the value of your research and, in doing so, constructing an argument may be summarised by posing some very basic questions, which should be addressed in designing any research activity which is intended to be of value to the rest of the world. Figure 2 details these basic questions in flow chart form and suggest an order for approaching them.

In practice, you should already have considered these questions in choosing your subject and judging the value and feasibility of the proposed topic. The 'what' and 'why' questions should help you to assess the inherent research value of your subject, the 'how' question should enable you to determine whether and in what way the research may be accomplished within the limits of your time and resources.

Having a clear idea of these questions at the beginning is not only essential for choosing a viable and worthwhile subject to research, but is also very useful in allowing you to map out the shape and direction of your research over the coming months. It provides you with valuable signposts to enable you to keep to the route that you have set for yourself, by acting as a reminder of your objectives and methods. Your plan or design thus serves as an *aide-memoire* as you progress with your project so that you can remind yourself:

▶ What is the scope and what are the boundaries of my subject? Am I straying beyond the proper field of my enquiry? Are my chosen boundaries still sensible and relevant and do I need to redefine the area of my research, and would that be possible within the time that I have?

▶ What are my objectives? How do I justify working in this field and what are my more exact purposes? Have I explained my argument clearly? Are my objectives sensible given the field of activity I have defined for myself?

▶ What are my methods? Are these appropriate for the subject and the objectives of the research? Are they feasible methods in view of my time and resources ?

Asking these questions at the beginning (when you may not yet have the answers) and constantly reminding yourself of them as the research progresses should enable you to demonstrate and judge the rigour of your research activity.

A careful and full consideration of these questions will also provide you with something else – when written down, these questions and answers should supply you with the best part of an introductory chapter to your thesis, in which you define the scope of your research and explain your objectives and methodology. You may find it useful to sketch out such a chapter as soon as possible, firstly to provide you with a written checklist of what you are doing, and why, and how, but also to give you some confidence about writing up the research by feeling that you have actually made a start on that activity, so that it does not loom ahead of you in an intimidating way as the research progresses.

Putting your ideas in context

In defining and justifying your proposed research you will also inevitably find yourself locating your project in the broader field of your subject. In explaining why your research is worthwhile, it will be necessary to point to gaps or unanswered questions in the existing body of learning and attempt to show how you intend to deal with this deficit. This part of the exercise should find expression in the part of your thesis which reports on the existing state of research and literature in the relevant field. This is likely to be an essential part of your argument and it will also be of help to the reader of your thesis to have a summary of what work has been done so far, and to cross-refer to details of this in a bibliography.

Working with your supervisor

Much of the designing and planning of research will be done in consultation with your supervisor, who may ask you to address the above questions and produce a draft outline of research activity. It is the role of the supervisor to help test your ideas about the value and feasibility of your research subject and then to advise you about appropriate approaches and methods. While this is often appreciated very quickly by students, it may be less easy to determine more exactly how far the supervisor should go in this role of advice and assistance. If at all in doubt on this issue, feel absolutely free to ask your supervisor for his or her own view of the role of supervision and what you may therefore expect in that respect. The requirements of supervision may vary according to subject and discipline; in some subjects, the student may be more easily left to his or her own devices in the library, in other areas the use of equipment or technology may require more detailed advice or supervision. Some institutions, or departments, may have written codes of practice or other notes of guidance, which explain the mutual expectations of supervisor and student. If these are available, ensure that you have a copy and that you are aware of what is laid down. This kind of documentation is helpful since it provides both students and supervisors with a clear idea of their respective roles and also gives the student something to wave at the less than diligent supervisor. In the absence of such clear general guidance it is important to clarify with your supervisor the extent of the supervisory role and you should certainly not feel any reticence in doing so.

Subject to what may be specifically provided in institutional or departmental codes or notes of guidance, or in degree regulations, there is a minimum level of advice you may generally expect from your supervisor. You may reasonably expect your supervisor

▶ to discuss your research ideas both as regards the subject and method of your proposed research, with a view to being given the go-ahead for your project

▶ to monitor your progress by responding to your own enquiries about how you should be proceeding with your research and by considering written reports or drafts of the thesis

▶ to advise on the standard of the written thesis by considering a draft and to alert you about any major omissions or defects in argument.

It is never easy to define precisely the limit of the supervisor's role. Obviously, the supervisor must take care not to 'take over' the student's work and become, in effect, the author of the thesis. But on the other hand, it would seem clear that the supervisor should guide the student around any major pitfalls. Your research effort should be independent but it is not expected that you can do absolutely everything for yourself.

Case studies

Adrian proves elusive

Adrian passed his examinations and other assessments comfortably, sometimes surprising the examiners with the depth of knowledge and degree of insight demonstrated in his written answers. Shortly before taking a break after the examinations he called to see a potential supervisor of his thesis and briefly but with a great deal of enthusiasm outlined an idea for his research. This was sufficient to convince the lecturer that Adrian had identified a worthwhile and interesting topic to work upon. Adrian then promised to submit a more detailed written proposal on his return from holiday two weeks later.

Four weeks later, Adrian's supervisor had neither seen nor heard anything from Adrian. The supervisor encountered him by chance outside the sports hall and asked him whether he had produced his draft thesis plan. Adrian explained that he had already completed the first part of his research and had accumulated 'a vast amount of material'. His supervisor expressed concern about the apparently unplanned nature of the research and insisted that they have a fuller discussion about objectives and methodology. An appointment was made for the following day.

Adrian failed to arrive for the meeting, but sent a note later that day explaining that he had been called away to an emergency meeting of the hockey club, but also enclosing a detailed bibliography of the works he had consulted so far. Another meeting was arranged for two days later, for which Adrian did appear with a draft outline of his research. They discussed Adrian's proposal for an hour and a half, with a number of amendments being made at the supervisor's suggestion: Adrian's plan was over-ambitious for a Master's thesis. He admitted that a good deal of the work he had already done will now have to be discarded, but cheerfully acknowledged that he now felt more confident about what he should be doing.

Nigel refuses to budge

Nigel was well ahead in his ideas for his thesis. After a seminar discussion earlier in the year he had approached the lecturer taking the seminar, saying that he thought one of the issues which had been debated gave rise to some significant questions which would serve as a good basis for a thesis. The lecturer agreed that there may be 'some mileage in the subject' and advised Nigel to contact him after the examinations to discuss the possibility further. Nigel felt convinced that the subject was ideal for his thesis and over the Easter break made a 5,000 word draft of the argument he wished to follow. He posted this to the lecturer, who replied that he had only had time to glance at the draft; however, it appeared to have some promise but he also indicated some probable methodological problems. He suggested that they come back to the subject after the examination period.

Slightly resentful at what he felt was a rebuff, Nigel pursued his ideas further at week-ends during the examination period. The day after his last examination he requested an interview with the lecturer whom he now called his supervisor and insisted on presenting a defence of his proposed methodology. This led to a somewhat testy interchange, with the supervisor (as he now was) continuing to express doubts about Nigel's approach. Nigel became increasingly taciturn during this interview and departed, agreeing 'to give some thought' to the supervisor's comments.

Samantha agonises about her ability

The examination period had been very stressful for Samantha, although her results were consistently strong. But even before the examinations she had approached one of the professors in her department, explaining that she was starting to worry about the thesis and doubting whether she 'had the intellectual equipment for that sort of thing' and that she had a number of ideas, although they were all probably rubbish. The professor assured her that some of her ideas sounded extremely interesting and that he would be very pleased to discuss them further after the examinations. In the meantime he urged her to stop worrying at this stage about the thesis.

Samantha returned to discuss the thesis after the examinations and, after looking at three possible topics, the professor agreed to supervise one of the proposed subjects. Samantha again expressed doubt about her ability to complete the research – she said that she had never tried to write anything as long as 20,000 words and she was only capable of writing short reports. She was also worried about stating the obvious and she was sure there could not be much worthwhile in her research proposal, because 'why else hasn't somebody already worked on this if it's that good?'. Her supervisor patiently asked her to repeat her basic objectives and outline her area of research, which she did immediately with extreme clarity and concision. He said adamantly that he was quite happy with her proposal, but she left, running her hand through her hair and saying 'My God, I sometimes wonder why I ever started this!'

Discussion points

1. What skills do you think you will be able to develop in the process of carrying out research and writing up a thesis at Master's level?

2. Are you able to quantify the time available for the work to be done on your thesis? What allocation of time would you suggest for the main phases of activity required for producing the thesis?

3. Can you list the main questions which ought to be addressed in constructing an outline of a Master's research project and how would you incorporate these questions into a model outline or plan for a Master's thesis in your field?

Questions and answers

Q. *I am unsure about the way in which the thesis fits into the overall scheme of study for the Master's degree and how to go about deciding on the subject matter of the thesis and arranging the supervision. How do I find out about this?*

A. It may be that your university or department (or both) have documentation, relating to your degree scheme or of a more general nature, dealing with the structure of the course and the procedures for arranging supervision, and any detailed information in a code of practice or degree scheme documentation could make all this clear to you. In the absence of sufficient guidance in this form, you should approach the member of staff in your department who has responsibility for the degree programme, or your personal tutor, director of studies or mentor if you have been allocated to a member of staff for such individual guidance. If you are at all unsure about how the degree programme is organised or delivered, you should feel confident, at any stage during the course, about approaching appropriate staff in the department in order to resolve these uncertainties. Remember to check notice-boards, your mail box and/or email, to avoid missing meetings. Check with secretarial staff if you are unsure which members of academic staff to approach.

Q. *How do I know whether my ideas for research are sensible and realistic, and whether I am hitting the right level in my research work?*

A. Both your proposal and plans for the research and the research activity itself should be discussed with your supervisor and he or she should monitor your progress. Your department will not allow you to proceed with the research without supervision, so that in effect you will need your supervisor's approval of your plans and willingness to supervise the subject you have chosen. The process of supervision should also alert you to the appropriate standard of research activity and academic writing for purposes of a Master's thesis. If you are at risk of seriously going astray this should be evident to you from your supervisor's comments and your supervisor should be ready to offer constructive advice. At a postgraduate level you are assumed to be capable of a fair measure of independent work, but you are not completely on your own – otherwise there would be no point in having any supervision.

Q. *I have been working for some time on my research but do not have a comfortable relationship with my supervisor. I am not sure whether this arises from a difference in temperament, or from problems in communicating with and understanding each other when we discuss my work, but the outcome is that I feel that my supervisor has a low opinion of me and this is undermining my confidence. What can I do about this situation?*

A. It is not always possible to achieve an ideal match between supervisor and student, either in terms of personality or even in the level of interest in and enthusiasm for the subject of the research. Something less than perfection may well have to be tolerated in practice on both sides! Unfortunately, however, in some cases a mismatch of personality or other instances of disagreement can sometimes develop into an irretrievably sour relationship which then threatens the viability of the thesis exercise. In such a case there should be departmental procedures in place for finding alternative supervision. Usually an approach should be made to either the degree programme co-ordinator, personal tutor or mentor (if allocated) or perhaps the head of department. If the department's documentation does not make it clear what to do in such a case, request a confidential meeting with any of the above persons. But consider the situation carefully and whether it may be little more than a problem of over-sensitivity – both students and academics can be notoriously sensitive about criticisms made of their work!

2

Understanding the Role of Theory
Colin Wight

One-minute summary – The aim of this chapter is to provide a brief introduction to theory and to explain its role in the research process. Whenever you undertake research you are already using theory even if you do not know it. Scientists routinely use theoretical concepts and generally have a clear idea of what makes a piece of research scientific, even if they have never explicitly thought about these issues. Out of the mass of available data the researcher has to select the most important factors and theory guides this process. Researchers use theory differently in different types of research, but some type of theory is present in all research. This chapter will help you to understand the key elements of theory and will be structured under the following headings:

► the role of theory
► key terms and the elements of theory
► main approaches to social theory
► putting it into practice.

The role of theory

Suppose you were talking to a friend about racial conflict. Suppose also that you and your friend agree that people learn negative stereotypes about other racial groups from their friends and families. This seemingly casual discussion is using a very basic theory to understand a social phenomenon. As this example shows people routinely use theories without making them explicit or labelling them as such. Politicians who claim that children raised by single mothers are more prone to crime are expressing a theory. Researchers engaged in the human genome project are using theories of DNA structure to guide their research.

Since all research involves some theory the question is not *whether* you should use theory, but *how* you should use it. Having an understanding of theory makes it easier to read and understand someone else's research and to conduct your own. An awareness of the role of theory in the research process helps clarify murky issues. Being explicit about theory leads to better designed, easier to understand and better conducted studies.

Theories help us to make sense of interrelated phenomena and in some instances can help us to predict the outcomes that are likely to occur when certain conditions are met. Researchers who connect their work to theory can generate better ideas about what to look for in a study and develop conclusions with more implications for further research. Building and evaluating theory is therefore one of the most important objectives of science. Theory is also important because it is easy for researchers to lose sight of the larger picture when conducting research. It is easy to focus on accumulating data rather than clarifying how the study fits into a more general understanding of the phenomena under study. So before, during and after a piece of research we need to continue to keep thinking theoretically.

Only the naïve researcher believes that theory is irrelevant to research or that a researcher just collects data. Researchers who attempt to proceed without theory or fail to make it explicit may waste time collecting useless data. They easily fall into the trap of vague and hazy thinking, faulty logic and develop and use imprecise concepts. Theory frames how we look at and think about a topic. It gives us concepts, provides basic assumptions, directs us to important questions and suggests ways for researchers to make sense of the data. But what is a theory? One common definition is that given in Figure 3.

A logically interrelated set of abstractions, ideas and propositions about empirical reality which organises knowledge about the world.

Figure 3. Theory.

For now this will suffice as a working definition, and would generally be accepted by most natural scientists. However, in the social sciences there is no real consensus on what theory is and we will consider alternatives in a later section.

▶ Theory is present in all research.

▶ Theory frames how we look at and think about a topic.

▶ Theory helps clarify how the study fits into a more general understanding of the phenomena under study.

▶ Theory can generate better ideas about what to look for in a study and develop conclusions with more implications for further research.

▶ Theory helps us to make sense of interrelated phenomena.

▶ Theory leads to better designed, easier to understand and better conducted studies.

Figure 4. Why use theory?

Key terms and the elements of theory

What do you think of when you hear the word theory? The word theory sometimes seems to scare students, and often with good reasons. Often theoretical language seems incredibly obscure and abstract. The mental picture many students have of theory is something that floats high among the clouds, a tangled web of jargon and abstractions that are irrelevant to the real world. Part of the problem is simply unfamiliarity with the language, but once the key terms are grasped there is no reason to treat theory as something only theorists do.

All theories possess some key elements and rest on a set of assumptions. The most important of these are the dreaded *ology* words: ontology, epistemology and methodology. Any word ending in *ology* simply means a science or critical analysis of that subject. Hence we have physiology, geology, mineralogy, and anthropology etc.

Ontology

Ont comes from the Greek word meaning 'to be' and ontology is the science of being, or existence. When philosophers talk of ontology they generally mean a systematic inquiry into the nature of existence itself. To a scientist, however the term takes on a slightly different meaning. All theories have an ontology, or to put it more simply, have an account of the phenomena under study and the relationships between these phenomena. This is the theory's ontology. The Watson-Crick theory of DNA structure, for example, claims that genes are made up of strands of material in the form of a double helix wound round one another about a common axis. This is an ontological claim about the nature of genetic material. Marx's theory of capitalist society suggests that there are dominant groups – the proletariat and the bourgeoisie – around which societal conflict occurs. This is a claim about the ontology of capitalist society. In this sense ontology simply refers to the assumptions about existence underlying any theory or piece of research. But there are different levels to a theory's ontology – the explicit and the implicit.

Concepts

Generally a theory's ontology will be explicitly expressed in terms of concepts. These concepts are ideas expressed in terms of symbols or words. In many natural sciences these concepts are often presented in symbolic form, such as formulae, or equations. Most social science concepts are expressed as words. Concepts are everywhere and you use them all the time, which only serves to illustrate that even in everyday life we theorise all of the time. The concepts we use in everyday life are often vague and unclear. Concepts used in research are much more rigorously defined and have very clear meanings. All theories require well-defined concepts.

Assumptions

As well as explicit and well-defined concepts another part of a theory's ontology are the implicit assumptions. Most natural scientists tend to work on the assumption that reality, or the objects of inquiry, exist independently of theories about them. Some quantum scientists and philosophers have challenged this assumption. Whether or not you think this a good assumption, the point is that it is an assumption which scientists rarely challenge. Think for example, about the concept of a book; this assumes a system of writing, people who can read and the existence of paper. It is possible to do research into the use of reference books in libraries and never think about these deeper assumptions. One way for a researcher to deepen his or her understanding is to identify the assumptions on which the concepts are based.

Methodology

Methodology is the science or critical study of methods. You will often see textbooks on research methods that discuss the use of a methodology. Strictly speaking this is incorrect. You use methods; methodology is the systematic assessment or study of those methods. It is important that you think about the most appropriate methods given the theory's ontology. Hence ontology and methodology are inextricably linked. In a sense methodological questions follow naturally from ontology. It is no use, for example, attempting to interview atoms, unless, of course, it is part of your theory's ontology that atoms can talk.

Epistemology

Epistemology is often the most troubling of these *ology* words, but it is quite a simple concept, although the implications of it are of major importance to researchers and hence it is often the subject of heated debate. As an ology it is clearly a science of something, and that something is derived from the Greek word for knowledge, *episteme*. Epistemology is simply the science, or critical study, of knowledge. Typical epistemological issues would be: the definition of knowledge; the sources and criteria for knowledge claims; the kinds of knowledge possible; the validity of knowledge claims; and the relationship between the knowledge claim and the object of knowledge.

From this you should be able to see why it is so important an issue. Research makes knowledge claims and researchers should be prepared to spell out on what basis those claims are made. It is always a valid question to ask of a researcher, 'which epistemology did you use?'. This allows other researchers to evaluate the research results and where possible to check them using the same data and methods and the same epistemology. However, another equally valid question is whether the chosen epistemology was appropriate to the object under study.

It is often assumed that science uses experience and observation as the basis of knowledge claims, and whilst this is generally true it is not always the case. Mathematics, for example, does not observe or experience that $2 + 2 = 4$. We know that $2 + 2 = 4$ through a process of logical reasoning, not experience or observation. Research that uses experience and observation is using an epistemology called *empiricism*. Research, such as mathematics, that uses logical reasoning is using an epistemology known as *rationalism*.

Although philosophers of science and social science spend much of their time debating the superiority of one epistemology over another, Einstein spelled out nicely the position adopted by most researchers. According to Einstein, scientists have to be epistemological opportunists adopting the basis of knowledge claims to suit the object under study.

More often than not scientists will use more than one epistemology to substantiate their research findings. Take for example the way we experience a stick that appears to be bent in water. Our experience seems to tell us that the stick is bent in the water yet straight when out. But we know this is not the case and in this example we use rationalism – our faculties of reasoning – to make sense of what we experience. What this example also shows is the manner in which experience can deceive us. Because of examples like this scientists generally take a sceptical stance to all knowledge claims and actively seek out many different forms of evidence using different epistemologies.

Main approaches to social theory

Although the above discussion may have convinced you of the importance of theory in research it has been based on a one-dimensional view of theory. This view may suffice for students in the natural sciences, but social science students need to be aware of some additional issues. Put simply, many social scientists argue that the ontology of the social world is so radically different from that of the natural world that a different view of theory is required. Other social scientists take a different view and argue that it is possible to theorise about the social world in the same way as we theorise about the natural world, and that we can use the same methods to study both. However, whatever the differences between these approaches, theories in both the natural and social science will inevitably contain the elements discussed above.

Positivist social science

Positivism was a theory of science that gained prominence in the twentieth century. The term positivist is generally used to mean an approach to the social sciences that models itself on the natural sciences. However, students should be wary of this term since one can believe in the scientific study of society without accepting the positivist theory of science. Positivists base their account of science on an empiricist epistemology and tend to prefer quantitative data and often use experiments, surveys and statistics. They seek rigorous, exact measures and objective research and they test hypotheses by carefully analysing numbers. Critics argue that positivism treats people as little other than numbers and that its concern with abstract laws and formulae are not relevant to the actual lives of real people.

Interpretative social science

Interpretative theorists argue that the positivist theory of science cannot be applied to the social sciences because the objects of social science are so radically different. According to interpretative theorists, such as Max Weber, the social sciences need to study meaningful social action. This approach argues that simple observation will not enable us to distinguish a blink from a wink. Although the outward signs of blinking and winking are the same, winking differs from blinking in that it is intentional. Hence these theorists argue that we must learn the personal reasons or motives that shape social behaviour. According to this approach, researchers conduct research to uncover the meanings embedded within social phenomena. When studying social events researchers need to get inside the social event in order to understand it. This is a radically different view of the relationship between the researcher and the object of inquiry from that of natural science.

Case studies: Putting theory into practice

Jane puts theory into practice

Jane considers this all irrelevant. She is interested in studying subatomic particles and can see no benefit in theory. One way to see how theory help shapes her research is to consider the nature of matter. Since the time of the ancient Greeks there have been theories about matter. If Jane been conducting her research then it would have been very different – if in fact a woman would have been allowed to conduct research. Ideas about matter have changed substantially since then, but some key moments stand out. A radical reformulation of the theory of atoms and classical physics resulted from the discovery of radioactivity by Becquerel in 1896, quantum theory, formulated by Planck in 1901 and the acceptance of the general theory of relativity, formulated by Einstein in 1916. Among other things scientists had to give up the ideas of:

1. the atom as the smallest, indivisible unit of matter

2. the unchangeable material identity of atoms and

3. the principle that it should be possible (in theory at least) to calculate and predict exactly the behaviour of single atoms.

And Jane, at least insofar as she follows these dominant theories, will have given up on these as well. So theories are shaping her research and an awareness of theory can be suggestive of further areas of research. For example, if atoms were the smallest indivisible unit of matter as we once thought, there would be little point in Jane looking for subatomic particles. Equally, Jane could attempt to challenge contemporary theories by trying to prove that these ideas should not have been discarded. So, for example, she could well attempt to show how it might be possible to calculate exactly the behaviour of single atoms. To do this, however, she will still need a theory to guide her research, perhaps one she develops herself.

Tom's research dilemma

Tom is interested in studying the role played by public opinion in shaping the attitude of government elites to poverty. He is worried about how he would go about researching such a topic and how he could ever prove his findings. There are various theoretical options available to Tom. He could, for example, simply observe levels of public concern about poverty and relate this to the policy outputs of state agencies. The problem with this approach is that it would be very difficult to say that we really 'knew' (the question of epistemology) that it was public concern about poverty that was driving the policy outputs. To get around this problem Tom might consider taking an interpretative approach to the issue and conduct interviews with policy makers to discover their attitudes and whether these change in relation to public opinion. Equally, Tom is going to have to come up with theoretical accounts of public opinion, poverty, and policy elites. And different theories will conceptualise these differently. Tom is going to have to be theoretically aware to ensure that he has coherent concepts of his entire cluster of variables and a clear theoretical understanding of how they relate to one another.

Catherine's lack of theory

Catherine is interested in exploring the constitution of adult sexuality as determined by the interaction of genetic constitution *and* the environment. She is aware that one theory which attempts to explain just this is epigenetic theory (the study of mechanisms involved in the production of phenotypic complexity in morphogenesis). However, research using this theory is generally carried out in medical schools or biological sciences and Catherine is interested in the 'social' mechanisms. This is a difficult one. The social sciences tend to be wary of any attempt to introduce a biological aspect to the explanation of social behaviour. Also, this type of research was discredited as a result of the practice of eugenics during the Second World War. There are clearly ethical and political issues raised in such research. However, since Catherine is interested in exploring the social mechanisms relating to adult sexuality, this shouldn't present too much of a problem. The big problem is going to be finding a supervisor who knows enough about epigenetics in a social science department. Catherine's best bet is to find a research centre that can supply expertise in both fields. The importation of theory from one field to another, however, is not easy, since disciplines tend to have fairly clear ideas of the kinds of research they consider appropriate.

Discussion points

1. What kinds of things are you interested in studying? How do they relate to other closely related phenomena, and what aspect of them do you wish to study?

2. What are the current competing theories in your field? What alternative avenues of research do they suggest?

3. How do theories come to dominate certain disciplines?

Questions and answers

Q. *My supervisor is firmly committed to a particular theory, but I have my doubts. I value the opinion of my supervisor, but I want to challenge some of his research findings. What should I do?*

A. This is often a worry for new students, but in general supervisors like nothing better than to be challenged. From their perspective every attempt to falsify a theory can serve as an instance of confirmation. One famous philosopher of science, Karl Popper, even suggested that the attempt to falsify theories was what science is. If however, your supervisor is totally unsupportive you may have to think about changing supervisors.

Q. *I have no idea how to set about studying my topic. I also don't want to spend large amounts of time ploughing through different theories. What can I do?*

A. First of all, speak to your supervisor, other researchers and other students. From this you should be able to gauge which are the dominant theories at present. This doesn't mean that you have to follow them, but it should narrow the field. Alternatively, scan the latest textbooks to see what the current state of theoretical development is in your field. Go to conferences and talk to people. You'll soon get a feel for where the action is and what interests you and what doesn't.

Q. *I want to study voting behaviour, but there are so many theories and they all seem to make some sense. How do I go about comparing them?*

A. This is one of the most difficult of all questions. The short answer is that there are many different theories about whether you can compare theories. These range from those that say theories can be compared to those that say they can't, and of course, positions in between. This doesn't seem to help much, does it? My advice is that if you want to compare theories you will need to ensure that you have a good theoretical defence of theory comparison in your dissertation. Don't, however, fall into the trap of attempting to answer the question of whether theories can be compared. This isn't what you are interested in. Leave this difficult question to the philosophers of science – they need something to do.

3

Constructing and Interpreting Qualitative Data
Mark Goodwin

One-minute summary – Depending on your subject area, your Master's thesis may well be based on an examination of qualitative data. This chapter will take you through the main methods used by researchers to construct and interpret such data. In doing so, it will cover the following areas:

▶ the nature and use of qualitative data
▶ the construction of qualitative data
▶ the interpretation of qualitative data.

The nature and use of qualitative data

Qualitative data allow us to investigate people's beliefs, values and actions. They allow us to examine the meanings of social activities and enable us to place these in a proper social context. They are non-numeric, and may consist of words, pictures, sounds or symbols. They are used to investigate particular research problems, such as those where we want to understand how and why particular events and actions happen and where we want to know how people feel about such activities. Often qualitative data are viewed as something separate from quantitative data, and the two are held to be quite distinct, requiring their own unique methods and approaches. Some students believe that the two types of data should not be mixed, and feel they have to choose between one and the other. This is, however, somewhat misleading, as the two types of data will often be used in the same research project and you may well need to use both in your own thesis. A project examining training schemes for the unemployed, for instance, may well use quantitative data to assess the level and extent of economic activity in a particular area, and then use qualitative data to investigate how people feel about the training schemes they have been on.

The misconception that the two types of data are quite separate is strengthened by the belief that each has its own methods, and that once you have chosen which type of data you require, you are necessarily restricted in the methods you can use. This again is untrue – the same method can be used to generate both quantitative and qualitative data. You can use a questionnaire to ask people how often they go shopping (generating quantitative material) and you can also ask them what they feel about the experience (generating qualitative data). You can watch how people behave in a meeting, or in a classroom (generating qualitative data) and

21

you can count the number of times they put their hands up (generating quantitative data). The point is that the two types of data should not be seen as distinctly separate. The key test is appropriateness – you must choose a research method that will generate the type of research data you need, to answer the research questions that you have set. The research problem comes first, the type of data appropriate to it comes second, and the type of method you use to generate that data comes third. Always work from research question, to data type, to method.

Table 1 is taken from Andrew Sayer's book on method in social science. It is useful because it summarises how different types of research design ask different sorts of questions, how they define their research objectives differently and how they use different research techniques and methods. Thus the difference between extensive and intensive research is not simply one of scale or breadth. It is one which affects all elements of the research process. Qualitative data will be more appropriate to addressing questions posed by intensive research where the aim is to understand the generation of particular processes and meanings in a small number of cases.

Table 1 Intensive and extensive research

	Intensive	*Extensive*
Research question	How does a process work in a particular case or small number of cases? What produces a certain change? What did the agents actually do?	What are the regularities, common patterns, distinguishing features of a population? How widely are certain characteristics or processes distributed or represented?
Relations	Substantial relations of connection.	Formal relations of similarity.
Type of groups studied	Causal groups.	Taxonomic groups.
Type of account produced	Causal explanation of the production of certain objects or events, though not necessarily representative ones.	Descriptive representative generalisations, lacking in explanatory penetration.
Typical methods	Study of individual agents in their causal contexts, interactive interviews, ethnography. Qualitative analysis.	Large-scale survey of population or representative sample, formal questionnaires, standardised interviews. Statistical analysis.

| Limitations | Actual concrete patterns and contingent relations are unlikely to be 'representative', 'average' or 'generalisable'. Necessary relations discovered will exist wherever their relata are present, e.g. causal powers of objects are generalisable to other contexts as they are necessary features of these objects. | Although representative of a whole population, they are unlikely to be generalisable to other populations at different times and places. Problem of ecological fallacy in making inferences about individuals. Limited explanatory power. |
| Appropriate tests | Corroboration | Replication |

Source: Sayer (1992) p. 243

The construction of qualitative data

Because qualitative data deal with feelings, beliefs, values and emotions, they are largely unstructured. In other words, they are not sitting around neatly waiting to be collected by the researcher – they have to be constructed. Moreover, qualitative data are often constructed as part of a research process which directly involves other people as elements in that process – these data come from talking to people, from interviewing them, from watching and observing them or from discussing things with them in groups. Whatever method is used, the construction of qualitative data has to be seen as a social activity, not as a neutral or technical procedure. And because you will be dealing with other people in a social situation, the generation of qualitative data can be quite challenging and exciting as well as complex and difficult. It is not the easy option for those who simply wish to avoid encountering statistics – the methods that are employed to construct qualitative data have to be used in a rigorous and proper manner if those data are to be reliable and meaningful.

There is a range of different methods you can use to generate qualitative data – as mentioned before, the critical thing is to ensure that you decide on the ones that are appropriate for generating the type of data you need to address your particular research questions. No method is either right or wrong at the outset – they will simply be more or less appropriate for constructing data that are relevant to your particular thesis.

A more helpful distinction to draw (than the one between qualitative and quantitative data) is perhaps the one between data you have to construct as the researcher, and data which has already been constructed for you. Again, your thesis will probably involve a mixture of the two. Table 2 below gives you an idea of the range of sources and methods that can be used to generate each type of data.

Table 2 Sources of data

Pre-constructed data	Research-constructed data
Official data	Interviews
Academic reports/books	Participation and observation
Research reports	Questionnaires
Media output	Panels/focus groups

Essentially, all qualitative data can be constructed from one of three broad methods:

1. **Questioning** (or talking to people). The methods under this heading range from the standard questionnaire, used many times in the same format, to the one-off interview which is completely unstructured.

2. **Observation** (or watching people). These methods range from hidden observation to full participation.

3. **Documentary research** (or reading). Again, a range of methods is used, drawing on material which is not just textual, but includes any material which provides information to the researcher, e.g. videos, photographs, and paintings.

We will now look in more detail at each of these three broad ways of constructing qualitative data. It should be made clear that these are not mutually exclusive – just as a single piece of research might draw on quantitative and qualitative data, it may well generate its qualitative data from a variety of sources. The issue is not so much having to choose between one method and another, but using all those which are able to produce appropriate data. The key is to restrict the scale and scope of the research to what can feasibly be conducted given the timescale and resources available. Indeed, it is precisely because all students will be affected by such restrictions that a mixture of different methods might prove effective. Since we have our own restrictions, i.e. space is limited, we will give an initial flavour of each technique, and provide a bibliography at the end of the book for those who wish to follow up and pursue particular methods in more detail.

Questioning and interviewing

This is perhaps the most common method of generating qualitative data. Indeed, talking to people is the most common way of gaining any information. The difference is that the techniques that are used inside research are rigorous and standardised. They range from the most formal questionnaire, where every respondent is asked the same question in the same order in the same way, to the unstructured interview, where the respondents themselves are left to guide the flow of conversation.

The questionnaire is often used to generate quantitative data but it can also act as a means of uncovering more qualitative information. In either case it will be used to survey a relatively large number of respondents with very specific questions. Even where qualitative data are sought, these will often be analysed in a quantitative manner. You could for instance use a questionnaire to determine the attitudes of the residents of a village about their reaction to a new bypass. You could ask them to grade their views about the bypass, from very necessary to totally unnecessary, and then quantify the results. In this way, attitudinal data which is qualitative can be analysed and presented in a quantitative manner. The purpose of the questionnaire is usually to undertake extensive research, seeking broad patterns of thought and behaviour within a sample population.

Other types of qualitative data do not lend themselves to quantification, since they concern the views and beliefs of individuals or small groups. The purpose is not to discover how many people share the same attitude (as with a questionnaire) but to uncover the meanings and intentions of specific actors in specific situations. In this instance, interviews will normally be used rather than questionnaires, since these offer a good means of examining experiences, feelings and values. You could, for instance, use interviews to find out from transport officials why they decided to build the bypass around that particular village, or you could interview road protesters about why they were trying to prevent the bypass from being built. In either case an interview would be an appropriate way of constructing the relevant data.

Interviews themselves, however, can vary in shape and form – again depending on what you need to know. As we noted before, interviews are social activities involving other people and as such they have a social dynamic which has to be taken into account. They amount to far more than simply asking questions, and you need to be aware of the different ways in which questions can be asked and the different strategies which can be followed during an interview. Some interviews are similar to extended questionnaires, where a set pattern of questions is worked out beforehand and then asked in a precise order. This is known as a structured open-ended interview. The difference between this and a questionnaire is that the replies are not specified around particular sets of responses, but are open-ended – hence the name. In other instances the researcher begins the interview with a broad idea of the topics they wish to cover (this is called the *interview schedule*) but is prepared to let the drift of the conversation dictate both the order and content of the specific questions. This is known as the semi-structured interview. In contrast to this, some interviews are almost completely unstructured – the researcher simply asks one or two questions at the beginning and then lets the interviewee structure the content and direction of the interview. This might be used, for instance, where you wish to uncover experiences and events which are significant

a) The Structured Open-ended Interview – to local residents

Preamble

I am interested in how you feel about the new bypass and wish to ask you a series of questions about this. Your answers will be treated in the strictest confidence.

Questions

1. How does the bypass affect you personally?
2. In which ways do you feel the bypass might help or hinder the journeys you make?
3. How do you think the bypass might affect the local environment?
4. Do you think the road might encourage more visitors to the area – if so which ones?
5. Do you think the council consulted you properly on the plans for the road?

b) The Semi-structured Interview – to members of a local residents association

Preamble

I am interested in how your association feels about the new bypass and wish to ask you a series of questions about this. I won't ask specific questions but do wish to cover a number of topics. Your answers will be treated in the strictest confidence.

Topics to be covered

1. When did they join the residents association?
2. Did they join because of the bypass?
3. What has been the attitude of the residents association?
4. How successful have been the actions of the association?
5. Do you link up with other groups?
6. How has the local council responded to you?

c) The Unstructured Interview – to members of an environmental protest group

Preamble

I am interested in why you joined this group, and what you feel you can contribute to the environmental movement through your actions in opposing this road. Could you just tell me how you first got started in environmental protests? Have you always had strong convictions against roads, for instance?

Topics to be covered

There is no predetermined agenda, and topics and questions simply arise from the flow of conversation.

d) The Focus Group – consisting of local councillors from one political party

Preamble

I am interested in how your party came to take the decision to go ahead with this bypass. I'd like to ask you all a few questions – please feel free to chip in and contribute when you feel you can add to what's being said.

Topics to be covered

1. What were original political party views on the road?
2. What is the extent of dissent?
3. How did they take the views of local residents into account?
4. How important were the views of the planners?
5. Were the views of your party in London important?
6. How do you think the protesters will affect progress?

Figure 5. Examples of interview types.

to the respondent, but which cannot be foreseen in advance, or where you need to gain a life history or biographical account. In some instances, interviews can be conducted with more than one person. Group interviews, or focus groups, are often used where the researcher is interested in the dynamics between the participants as well as in their individual responses. They can also be used where the responses of one person might encourage and stimulate responses from others. Figure 5 gives an example of each type of interview – note that each type is used to gain different types of information from different types of respondent.

Participating and observing

Qualitative data can also be gained from watching people as well as talking to them. Again, this type of method varies, depending on whether you are known to those you are observing, and on whether you are overt or covert in your research purpose. Possibilities range from complete participation to covert observation. In each case the object is for you as the researcher to be able to be present, and watch, as social events are unfolding around you. Your data comes from your own records and observations, not from the views of others. Hence the data comes from what people actually do (or your records of what they do) rather than from their recollections of what they did. Figure 6 gives a summary of the different ways of gaining data through participating and observing. The precise method that is chosen will depend on the nature of the research subject and on the level of access which is available. Full participation will allow you to share the lifestyles and experiences of those under study.

	External observation	Participant observation
Overt	Researcher does not conceal identity or purpose but does not participate in group under study.	Researcher does not conceal identity or purpose and participates in group under study.
	E.g., observes protest actions at bypass from vantage position at side of road.	E.g., works for local authority on a placement and observes road policies from within.
Covert	Researcher conceals identity and purpose but does not join any group under study.	Researcher joins group under study but does not tell them his/her purpose.
	E.g., observes protest actions at road by walking along public footpaths.	E.g., joins bypass protest movement as a full member but does not reveal research purposes.

Figure 6. Gaining data through participating and observing.
Source: Kitchin and Tate (2000) p. 220

But just as interviewing amounts to far more than simply asking questions, observation amounts to far more than simply watching other people. Full participation involves the building of trust and acceptance. Overt observation involves the ability to record and detail information in difficult situations. In either case you will be faced with a decision about what to record and what to leave out – in other words you have to decide on the spot what is likely to be relevant and important data and what is not. Figure 7 contains a number of useful tips for undertaking observational studies.

▶ Remember there is no such thing as just observing. A lens may have a centre and a periphery but it must be pointed somewhere.

▶ Review constantly what you are looking for, in terms of whether or not you are seeing it.

▶ Observation is necessarily an averaging out process and there will inevitably be times when you cannot sustain your attention.

▶ Try to assess what you are recording and why in terms of your research questions, rather than in terms of what appears obvious to the eye. What are you observing and why?

▶ Reflect critically on how you record the data in the field, and on your subsequent practices of writing that data up. Are you writing too much or too little?

Figure 7. Useful tips for undertaking observational studies.
Source: Kitchin and Tate (2000), 224, after Wolcott (1995) 96-101.

Documents and texts

So far we have concentrated on data that is constructed by the researcher. By turning our attention to documents and texts as a source of qualitative data we can now look at materials which have already been constructed by others. As might be expected there is a vast range of data available from such sources. These might be in the form of written text, but might also include for instance, electronic media, paintings, literature, photographs and architecture. The rule is not to restrict yourself to the most obvious documentary sources, but to use whichever 'texts' offer appropriate data to address your research questions. In addition to taking different forms, documentary sources have been constructed by others for all sorts of purposes. Those of potential interest to the researcher as a source of qualitative data might include personal documents, such as diaries and letters; official documents, such as minutes of local authority meetings, or memos from a health authority; imaginative documents, such as poems or paintings; and corporate documents, such as company records and annual reports. There are a number of advantages in using documents to construct qualitative data. These are listed below in Figure 8.

▶ They can open up relatively inaccessible worlds – a famous study of Polish peasants migrating to the USA (Thomas and Znaniecki, 1927) was based on five groups of documentary data; letters to families and friends in Poland; a life history of one particular peasant; a collection of newspaper articles from Polish archives; a set of documents from social agencies in Poland and the USA; and a series of third person reports, gleaned from social work agencies and court records.

▶ Documentary sources can also open up social worlds which, though accessible in principle, are actually relatively closed. Davis (1990) has used a variety of newspaper reports, police documents and verbatim records of televised interviews to look at the military-style policing of contemporary Los Angeles, with particular reference to the so-called 'war on drugs'.

▶ Documentary sources offer the possibility of conducting historical and longitudinal studies, over a long time series.

▶ In a similar manner, just as they can be used to compare events across time, documentary sources can be used to analyse cross-cultural processes – comparing data from across a range of countries.

▶ Documentary materials are potentially very cheap and often easy to access. The researcher does not have to pay huge sums of money setting up research teams in a quest for material. The sources are often available in a record or reference library, and they are often collected together in a useable form.

Figure 8. The advantages of documents as sources of qualitative data.

What all documentary sources have in common is that they have been constructed for other purposes. Their primary purpose is not to provide research data, but it is important for the researcher to appreciate why and how they were initially constructed. As Hammersley and Atkinson put it, (1984, p.137) 'rather than being viewed as a (more or less biased) source of data....documents....should be treated as social products: they must be examined, not simply used as a resource. To treat them as a resource and not a topic is to....treat as a reflection or document of the world phenomena that are actually produced by it'.

Thus we have to try to establish the purpose behind the production of the document rather than just accept the record as somehow 'given'. Documents are not impartial and autonomous accounts of particular events and processes, instead they must be seen as integral to the institution, agency or individual which produced them. There are a number of other potential difficulties involved in using documents. It is not a matter of simply taking interesting looking reports off a shelf and noting their contents. Scott (1990) sets out four key criteria involved in the use of documentary sources. These are listed below in Figure 9.

> ▶ Authenticity – is the source of the document correctly attributed?
>
> ▶ Credibility – is the source accurate and was it recorded with sincerity?
>
> ▶ Representativeness – is the source representative of opinion at that time and place? Are there alternative sources which might be used?
>
> ▶ Meaning – can the source be used in a literal sense, or is some level of interpretation required to understand the purposes of the recorder?

Figure 9. Assessing the validity of documentary data. *Figure constructed from text in Scott (1990)*

Sampling and selecting respondents

Whatever method of data construction is felt to be most appropriate, the researcher will have to select carefully those sources that can provide the most relevant information. To some extent this is fairly straightforward, as qualitative data is often used to explore purposeful activity or emotions in a limited number of cases. Thus, to understand how local residents feel about the construction of a bypass, the researcher will need to approach those living near the new road. Even in this instance however, limited time and resources may mean that the researcher can only take a sample of opinion rather than gather it from the whole population. A village of 500 homes will be too much for a Master's student to survey in its entirety, but a 10% sample of 50 respondents should be possible. The issue concerns which 50 – should they be selected at random, or should they include certain numbers of specified groups to ensure a coverage of elderly residents or new residents, or men and women, or car owners and non-car owners?

But things are rarely even this simple, and sometimes the researcher will have to spend time identifying the most relevant respondents. Difficulties arise, for instance, when the focus of research is on the actions or decisions of an institution. Who inside that institution should be approached? If the research question is to account for the siting of the bypass, rather than to analyse how local residents feel about it, this immediately raises additional questions. Who should be approached within the local authority which gave the go-ahead – the planners, the surveyors, the transport engineers? Should research concentrate on council officials or elected councillors? Should external agencies such as transport pressure groups, or environmental activists be approached? How local should the research be, or will the researcher need to consult regional and national organisations? These are all questions which arise at the outset of the research. Answering these goes hand-in-hand with choosing appropriate methods. Thought should be given to more than just how the research is to be undertaken – attention also needs to be paid to who the precise subjects of the research will be, and to which individuals, say, or groups, or sets of documents, or collections of paintings, will provide the most relevant sources of data.

Interpreting qualitative data

As even this brief overview will have shown, qualitative data comes in many guises. It is rarely neat and ordered, and therefore a special importance must be placed on how such data is interpreted. In many ways constructing and generating the data is only the beginning of the research process. An equally large task is to analyse and make sense of the data. This is difficult, of course, because data never speak for themselves – they have to be interpreted by the researcher. When you return from fieldwork you will be faced with a collection of disparate and partial pieces of information – some relating to events, some to feelings, some given by individuals in an interview, some gathered from 50 respondents via a questionnaire. Your task is to pull all of this together in a meaningful way so that your research questions can be investigated and answered.

Although it is difficult to be precise about the analysis of qualitative data because each research problem will generate different amounts and types of data, Dey (1993) has provided us with a very general scheme of interpretation. He maintains that all qualitative data will have to undergo three stages of analysis – they will have to be described, classified and then connected. Description simply involves the portrayal of data in a form which can be analysed – for qualitative data this is mainly textual. Thus interviews will normally be recorded, and the recording word-processed as an interview transcript. This gives a verbatim record of what was said by all parties during the interview. Notes and records from observational fieldwork will usually be written up in the form of a research diary. Material from documents will usually have been recorded in note form, or may exist as complete photocopies for instance. To a certain extent, at this first stage of the analysis the data will be in a fairly raw form. It therefore needs organising and classifying.

This is the point at which we enter the next stage of classification. The jumble of data has to be put in order and sifted and sorted into meaningful sets of data. Classification necessarily involves breaking up your data and moving it around. If you had ten interview transcripts with different local government officers all on the theme of the siting of the bypass, you might wish to identify all their answers which mentioned the role of central government. These could then be extracted from their individual interviews, and placed alongside one another to gain an overall impression of what people considered to be the level of central involvement in the building of the road.

The third stage is termed connection. For Dey this involves more than just identifying similarities between different categories of data. It involves analysing the interconnections between different types of data. Dey uses a building analogy to clarify this. Whereas classification involves sorting all the bricks, windows, beams and frames into different piles, connection involves putting them together into a larger structure. These three stages are not necessarily linear – there will be iterative procedures to be made at each stage, reflecting back on what has gone before and making modifications as a result. Figure 10 is a representation of this process.

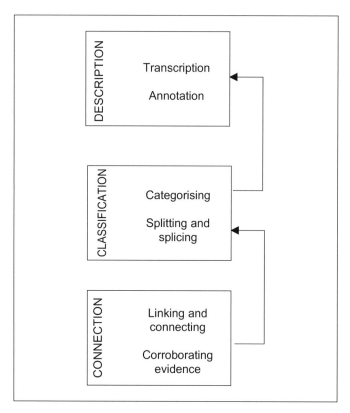

Figure 10. Description, classification and connection. *Source: Kitchin & Tate (2000)* p. 235.

This whole procedure is necessarily complex – it is, for instance, more difficult to sift and sort qualitative data into workable categories than it is for quantitative data, which do fall into ordinal, nominal, interval and ratio categories (as we will see in the next chapter). The categories to be used for qualitative data are not so straightforward, and have to be imposed by the researcher. The skill is to draw out the implications of different types of data, and connect them in a way which enables them to bear the weight of the interpretation which is placed upon them. In other words do not claim too much for your data, and only draw conclusions which you are able to substantiate. The thesis will suffer if you try to claim too much which you cannot give evidence for – or indeed if you do not make enough of your material. The trick is to recognise that your conclusions will only be as good as the data you generate to support them.

Case studies

Glenda writes a letter

Glenda has planned her research project and knows that she wishes to interview a range of local businesspeople on their attitudes to the local bypass. However, she does not know how to go about this. The easiest way is to write letters asking for an interview – but to whom should she write? Glenda remembers some important advice that she should always identify an appropriate sampling frame from which to draw potential respondents. Since she hoped to interview businesspeople, Glenda decided to look through a commercial directory, or index, along with the *Yellow Pages* telephone directory. Having done this, she drew up a list of names and addresses of potential interviewees. At the next stage, Glenda decided how many people she needed to interview in order to gain the necessary data. She then decided on a sampling strategy to select this number from her entire list. Once she had done this she wrote her letters, remembering that they should be short, informative and above all polite. Glenda needed to gain 'in principle' permission to talk to those she had selected, but she also realised that the details of the meeting could be arranged and confirmed later, although she did feel it might be useful in the letter to suggest some dates, or even a broad timescale. She remembered to use headed paper, and gave details of where she could be contacted if further details were required. She prepared herself for a few disappointments – after all, those chosen as potential respondents will rarely all say yes, and Glenda would need to work on a contingency plan in case some key respondents refused.

Terry forgets the tape recorder

Terry has gone to interview a local resident about the new road. However, he is just about to begin the interview by asking if the interviewee minds being taped (consent is always vital) when he realises he has forgotten to bring his tape recorder. For a moment he panics, wondering how he will record all the data. Then he remembers he has a pencil and notepad, and he uses these to take down the main elements of what is said. He realises that he will not be able to use the data in quite the same way as if he had recorded it – he will not, for instance, be able to quote verbatim from the interview. He will, however, be able to state broadly what the views of the respondent were. On the way home he realises that this is a fairly common occurrence – he remembers other students who have told him how they forgot to turn the tape on, and how they did not bring enough tapes. As soon as he gets home he writes up the main points which were raised in the interview. He vows next time to go through his checklist of tape recorder, tapes, interview schedule, batteries, notepad and pencil a little more thoroughly.

Jane tries to interpret her data

Jane has worked hard to gather a range of data on the building of the new bypass. She has several interview transcripts, 100 questionnaire returns, notes of council meetings she attended as a member of the public, minutes of official meetings, and company reports from the firm that is building the road. She also has leaflets distributed by a protest group. Her problem is that some of these data sets seem to be telling her a different story to others. The road builders claim in their report that they have local support, yet her questionnaire survey and the protest group leaflet claim local opposition. The person from the council's planning department told her he was responsible for the siting of the road, yet the surveyors claimed they had responsibility. She remembered that one way of resolving, and indeed accommodating, these types of differences is through a technique called triangulation. Jane checked each source against the others, looking for inconsistencies. She noticed, for instance, that later in the company report it mentioned that their survey showing support for the road was carried out on a county scale. Therefore the villagers and the protest group could legitimately claim a more local opposition. She also noted that in the official council minutes of a transport committee meeting that the surveyors department was thanked for its lead role in siting the road. Jane had been able to build up an account of the road's development which fully matched the evidence she presented. She was pleased that she had not claimed too much or too little from her data.

Discussion points

1. Can you think of alternative ways of constructing the data that you need to address your research questions?

2. How should you choose between the use of questionnaires and interviews, and between the use of different types of interviews?

3. Why are documents a useful source of qualitative data?

Questions and answers

Q. *Can I mix qualitative and quantitative data in my thesis? I am worried because most text books treat these as completely separate.*

A. You are perfectly entitled to mix both quantitative and qualitative research. Indeed, in many projects this would be expected. The key point is that the two types of data are used to address different types of research questions – in this sense they are complementary rather than competing. You simply need to ensure that you are using the right data to address your research questions, and that you do not expect quantitative data dealing with broad regularities to answer questions about particular case studies which are better addressed through qualitative data.

Q. *I have been told I need 50 questionnaires. Is this a good number?*

A. How long is a piece of string? Fifty may be a useful number, and may generate the data you need, but it depends on the size of your 'total population'. If you were undertaking research on schoolchildren and wanted to look at the behaviour of one class of 30, it would be possible to cover the entire population in 30 questionnaires. On the other hand, if you were seeking to explore the attitudes of those living in a town of 5,000 to the closure of a local factory, then 50 may be too few. The general rule is to undertake as big a sample size as you can – within the obvious limits of time and other resources. And here we should insert a warning not to overstretch yourself. It also depends on how important the questionnaire data are to your overall study. If they are the key means of answering your research question, then the more the better. If they are only one source amongst many, then you may well have to limit the number in order to have the time to generate other types of data.

Q. *Should I record all my interviews? Will this make the interpretation of my data easier?*

A. It will and it won't! As a general rule, the clearer and cleaner the data, the easier the interpretation. This is why many researchers prefer to have all their data from interviews in a verbatim transcript. However, this is only absolutely necessary if you need to quote directly from the respondents. If you just want to gain a general impression of their views and attitudes, then your notes of the interview will be sufficient. As a word of warning it should be noted that interviews take a long time to transcribe, and this should be built into your research timetable. As a rough guide, most researchers would allow one day of interpretation for every day spent constructing data.

Analysing Quantitative Data
Alan Bond, John A. Brierley and Mark Tippett

One-minute summary – It may be that in the process of researching your Master's thesis, you generate some quantitative data which you need to analyse statistically so that you can see whether you can be confident about what the data is telling you. This chapter cannot hope to explain what the appropriate statistical techniques are for your purposes; rather the aim is to get you to think early on about your research design so that you produce data which can be analysed in a statistically meaningful way. There are some important measurement issues which you need to be aware of before embarking on empirical research, and some good advice can be given regarding research designed with statistical analysis in mind. This chapter will help you to start your research along the right lines with advice given under the following headings:

▶ explaining measurement rules
▶ explaining measurement scales
▶ designing research so that meaningful statistical operations can be applied.

Explaining measurement rules

There are certain rules for measurement which were originally set out by Stevens (1946) in an article which is widely recognised in the social sciences as being of great value. You may think that work produced as long ago as 1946 has had sufficient time to become accepted, and its recommendations adopted in today's research. In fact, this is often not the case! It is important that you become aware of the main features of Stevens' work so that you do not apply inappropriate statistical techniques to your data. If you do fall into this trap, you run the risk of reaching conclusions which, in reality, may have little or no supporting evidence. We need to start with a basic definition of the term 'measurement'. Box 1 provides the definition contained within the original article published by Stevens (1946).

Box 1 Definition of measurement

' ... the assignment of numerals to objects or events according to rules....'

So, for example, a measurement of length of one metre uses a system which has rules set by an international organisation called The General Conference on

Weights and Measures, and all the major countries of the world have a representative on this organisation. The rules are part of the Système International (SI) with which many of us will be familiar. It used to be that a measurement of one metre represented a standard length based on the length of a platinum-iridium alloy bar based in France. The difficulty with a rule of measurement like this is that reproducibility is difficult in other countries as lengths have to be calibrated against this one bar. For this reason, the standard length was changed in 1960 to be equivalent to the wavelength of orange-red light emitted by atoms of krypton-86. Hence, one metre is now defined as 1,650,763.73 times the wavelength of this kind of light. This explanation should illustrate that measurements can only take place according to rules which have been set, although in most cases you are probably completely unaware of the existence of such rules.

Measurement in its most general sense can be regarded as some form of *mapping* from a set of objects, events or properties, into some subset of the real numbers. There is a notation with which you need to be familiar in order to progress through this chapter. Take as an example the situation illustrated in Figure 11. You have two sets of numbers. Each number in the first set, called the domain, is associated with just one number in the second set, called the range. This association is a function or a mapping and, in this particular example, is simply the square function. Therefore, each number in the domain of the function is mapped to an associated number in the range of the function as shown in Figure 11.

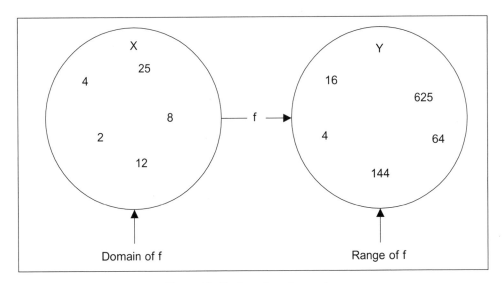

Figure 11. Explanation of mapping.

It is normal practice to refer collectively to the domain as X, the range as Y, and the functional relationship between them as a measurement rule. In other words, a measurement rule can be defined as in Box 2.

┌───┐
│   **Box 2 Definition of a measurement rule**   │
│   │
│ A measurement rule has three components: a │
│ domain (X) a range (Y) and a mapping (f) from X into Y. │
└───┘

Figure 11 is a simple mathematical example of a measurement rule. A more familiar example, however, is one where temperatures are recorded using the centigrade rule. With this example the measurement rule comprises a domain which contains the times at which the temperatures were taken, a range comprising the actual temperatures recorded at these times and a mapping from the domain to the range defined by the centigrade rule. Another example involves the assessment of relative intelligence for a given set of individuals. Intelligence is assessed by having individuals answer a standard set of questions with marks awarded to each question based on a rigidly defined marking rule. Hence, the measurement rule is comprised of a domain consisting of the set of individuals to which the test is applied, the range contains the intelligence scores they obtain based on a rule which awards marks based on a standard set of questions.

It is important to note, however, that measurement rules are often not unique; temperature, for example, can be measured using a variety of measurement rules and these rules will in general return different measures of the same temperature. For example, if we use the Fahrenheit rule we may come to the conclusion that the temperature at a particular time is 32 degrees. However, the same temperature measured on the centigrade rule is zero degrees. It is, of course, well known that once we have measured temperature using one rule it is easily converted to the 'equivalent' temperature implied by another rule. In the present example the relationship between temperature under the Fahrenheit rule (H) and the centigrade rule (C) is given by the formula $H = 32 + \frac{9}{5}*C$. However, the fact that we can use different rules to measure the same phenomena has some very important implications for the types of statistical procedures we can apply to the data that we end up using in our empirical work. We can summarise the issues this raises in terms of three crucial 'identification' criteria. Before conducting empirical work, researchers should therefore:

1. identify the measurement rules (admissible measurement procedures) appropriate to the empirical situation being investigated;

2. determine the group affiliation of the collection of measurement rules specified in (i); and

3. determine the 'statistical procedures' which may be *meaningfully* applied to the data they end up working with.

The importance of these identification issues can be demonstrated in terms of a simple numerical example. Imagine that we have two houses – house A and house

B. We have taken measurements of the temperature in these two houses using the centigrade rule once at 8 o'clock in the morning, and once at 5 o'clock in the afternoon on the same day. Table 3 sets out the results.

Table 3 House temperatures in degrees centigrade

House	Temperature at 8 a.m.	Temperature at 5 p.m.
A	2°C	10°C
B	4°C	6°C

We could also have taken measurements in Fahrenheit, or we could simply convert the temperatures to the Fahrenheit measurement rule using the standard formula, $H = 32 + \frac{9}{5}*C$ as in Table 4.

Table 4 House temperature in degrees Fahrenheit

House	Temperature at 8 a.m.	Temperature at 5 p.m.
A	35.6°F	50°F
B	39.2°F	42.8°F

Perhaps you wanted to know whether house A is hotter than house B. What you could do is calculate the geometric mean so that, for example, the two temperature measurements for house A were multiplied by each other, and the square root of the result gives the geometric mean, or $\sqrt{2 \times 10} = 4.47$. Table 5 sets out the results of this calculation using the centigrade measurement rule.

Table 5 House temperatures in degrees centigrade and their geometric mean

House	Temperature at 8 a.m.	Temperature at 5 p.m.
A	2°C	10°C
A	Geometric mean = 4.47°C	
B	4°C	6°C
B	Geometric mean = 4.90°C	

So, house B is hotter than house A. Or is it? Table 6 sets out the results of the same calculation using the Fahrenheit scale.

Table 6 House temperatures in degrees Fahrenheit and their geometric mean

House	Temperature at 8 a.m.	Temperature at 5 p.m.
A	35.6°F	50°F
A	Geometric mean = 42.19°F	
B	39.2°F	42.8°F
B	Geometric mean = 40.96°F	

Now house A is hotter than house B! It thus follows that the geometric mean is a *meaningless* statistic if applied to a temperature series; for a legitimate change in the measurement rule used may enable one to reach diametrically opposed statistical conclusions. It goes without saying that those interested in scholarly research would prefer to avoid problems like this!

Explaining measurement scales

Having set out the kinds of problems that can be encountered with quantitative analysis, this section goes on to identify the statistical operations which can meaningfully be applied to data. It should be emphasised that it is beyond the scope of this chapter to provide instruction on the statistical tools themselves. The aim of the chapter is simply to identify the appropriate statistical operations which can be applied to different measurement rules. Armed with this knowledge, you will be in a position to design research accordingly, and you will be able to seek advice more quickly regarding the application of the statistical tools you wish to use.

The first thing you need to know is the measurement scale you are dealing with and there is a definition which can help as indicated in box 3.

Box 3 Definition of measurement scale

The measurement rules f and g are J scaled if there exists a function π in J such that $g = \pi{*}f$. A measurement scale C_J is a collection of measurement rules which are mutually J scaled.

The definition contained in box 3 is rather technical and so, an example will be given here to explain what it means. In the measurement of temperature, for example, we can move between the centigrade (C) and Fahrenheit (H) measurement rules by merely applying the transformation $H = 32 + \frac{9}{5}{*}C$. This transformation is a member of the general linear group and so it follows from the above definition that the centigrade and Fahrenheit measurement rules are members of the scale defined by this group. However, note that whilst there is a linear relationship between temperatures based on the centigrade rule and

* See *Social Statistics* by Ian Hosker, published by Studymates ISBN 1-84285-004-0

temperatures based on the Fahrenheit rule, the temperature at which water freezes is different under the two rules. For the centigrade rule water freezes at a temperature of $0°C$, whilst for the Fahrenheit rule water freezes at $32°F$. In other words, the 'zero point', or the temperature at which water freezes is arbitrarily determined. Hence, Stevens (1946) suggests that instead of saying that temperature is defined on the general linear group scale, which is a bit of a mouthful, that we say instead that it is defined on the 'interval scale'. This is because the difference (or interval) between two temperatures does have a natural zero point. We can demonstrate this by considering the maximum and minimum temperatures on a given day which, for example, might amount to $14°C$ and $4°C$ respectively, based on the centigrade rule. It follows that the difference between the maximum and minimum temperatures is $10°C$. Under the Fahrenheit rule, however, the maximum temperature will be $57.2°F$ whilst the minimum is $39.2°F$. The difference between the maximum and minimum temperatures is therefore, $57.2 - 39.2 = 18°F$ if the Fahrenheit rule is used. But this could just as easily have been calculated by multiplying the difference between the maximum and minimum temperatures based on the centigrade rule by $\frac{9}{5}$, so that using the Fahrenheit rule, the difference between the temperatures is $10 \times \frac{9}{5} = 18°F$. It follows from this that if the difference (or interval) between two temperatures based on the centigrade rule is zero, then the difference between the two temperatures will also be zero if the Fahrenheit rule is used.

Stevens also suggested that there are three other measurement scales which are likely to be useful when handling data. They are displayed in Table 7. Note that each of these scales is defined by the group affiliation of the transformations which define the relationship between its measurement rules. Thus, in the Stevens scheme, measurement occurs on a nominal, ordinal, interval or ratio scale according to whether each pair of admissible measurement rules involves the determination of equality (the permutation group), determination of greater or less than (isotonic group), determination of equality of intervals or differences (general linear group) and the determination of equality of ratios (similarity group).

Table 7 The Stevens scales of measurement

Scale	Basic operations	Group structure (J)
Nominal	Determination of equality	Permutation group (any one-to-one substitution)
Ordinal	Determination of greater or less than	Order preserving group (any monotonic increasing function)
Interval	Determination of equality of intervals or differences	General linear group ($y = a + bx$)
Ratio	Determination of equality of ratios	Similarity group ($y = bx$)

This table is important because it categorises data into one of four scales. The next section will develop this further and will demonstrate how these scales can be used to determine whether particular statistical techniques are valid.

Designing research so that meaningful statistical operations can be applied

Taken by themselves, the measurement scales are a convenient device for classifying data according to the transformations which may be legitimately applied to them. Whilst this is important, their most important role is in determining the 'statistical procedures' which can meaningfully be applied to data defined in terms of a particular scale. This 'statistical meaningfulness' concept, which was in fact demonstrated in terms of the temperature data above, is defined mathematically in box 4.

Box 4 Definition of meaningful numerical procedures

A 'numerical procedure' Φ is said to be J($\sim$,f) scale meaningful if when $\Phi(f') \sim \Phi(f'')$ then $\Phi(\pi*f') \sim \Phi(\pi*f'')$ for all f', f'' in C_J and π in J.

Box 3 demonstrated that the J measurement scale C_J is a collection of measurement rules which are mutually J scaled. Box 4 develops on this and gives a technical definition from which we can work out when a statistical procedure can be correctly applied to data. In the box 4 definition, the tilde ($\sim$) simply represents one of the arithmetic operations 'greater than' ($>$), 'equivalence' ($=$) or combinations thereof ($\leq$ or $\geq$). The definition requires that, if a particular relationship holds between two sets of data, it should also hold if the data are transformed in a legitimate way; i.e., by using an alternative measurement rule. In the temperature example referred to earlier we show that the relationship between two geometric means can be changed (reversed) simply by restating data from the centigrade to the Fahrenheit rule. It thus follows that the relationship required for a statistic to be meaningful is violated and so we conclude that the geometric mean is a *meaningless* statistic if applied to data defined in terms of the interval scale.

The potential for problems of this kind are much greater in the social sciences where it can often be difficult, or even impossible, to define a unique unit of measurement. We can illustrate this by considering two sets of hypothetical data of IQ scores (measuring intelligence). In our example, we will consider two classes, class A and class B. Table 8 presents the results of the IQ tests taken by the hypothetical students in each class.

Table 8 Intelligence scores in two hypothetical classes

	Class A	Class B
Student 1	60	50
Student 2	94	100
Student 3	140	150
Average	$\dfrac{60 + 94 + 140}{3} = 98$	$\dfrac{50 + 100 + 150}{3} = 100$

The average intelligence score for class A is 98 whilst that for class B is 100. Hence, we might be tempted to think that 'on average' members of class A are less intelligent than members of class B. However, as with many intelligence assessment procedures, the unit of measurement is somewhat arbitrary and here, a higher score merely indicates that there is a higher level of intelligence; it says nothing about relative differences in intelligence. Hence, any order preserving (or isotonic) transformation may be applied to the data and from Table 7 this identifies the data as being defined on the ordinal scale. If, for example, we transform the data by taking the common logarithm of the 'raw' intelligence scores, we get a new set of intelligence measures as shown in Table 9.

Table 9 Common logarithm of intelligence scores in two hypothetical classes

	Class A	Class B
Student 1	$\log_{10}(60) = 1.778$	$\log_{10}(50) = 1.699$
Student 2	$\log_{10}(94) = 1.973$	$\log_{10}(100) = 2.000$
Student 3	$\log_{10}(140) = 2.146$	$\log_{10}(150) = 2.176$
Average	1.966	1.958

We can see that the average for the transformed data for class A is 1.966 whilst the average for class B is 1.958. Whilst the 'raw' data lead us to conclude that, on average, class B is more intelligent than class A, the transformed data lead us to exactly the opposite conclusion. This means that the average is a meaningless statistic if applied to data defined on the ordinal scale.

A summary of the meaningful statistical operations which can be applied to data defined on Stevens' four scales is detailed in Table 10. Suppose we have two sets of data, A and B, and that our calculations indicate that the variance (square of the standard deviation) of the group A data exceeds the variance of the group B data. If we transform both sets of data by a function from the general linear group, then Table 10 shows that the variance of the transformed data for group A will still exceed the variance of the transformed data for group B. Similarly, if the average for the group A data exceeds the average for the group B data, then Table 10 shows that the average of the transformed group A data will exceed the average of the group B transformed data. In other words, both the average and the variance are meaningful statistics if applied to data defined on the interval scale.

Furthermore, since the similarity group (of the ratio scale) is a special case of the general linear group (of the interval scale) in that it uses linear transformations with a unique zero (a is set equal to zero in the group structure which defines the ratio scale), then both the average and variance will also be meaningful statistics on the ratio scale. However, as the intelligence score example contained in Table 8, Table 9 and the surrounding discussion shows, neither the average nor the variance will be meaningful statistics for data defined on the ordinal or nominal scales. Similarly, whilst the median is a meaningful statistic for data defined on the ordinal scale, it is also a meaningful statistic for data defined on the interval and ratio scales. It is not, however, a meaningful statistic for data defined on the nominal scale. In other words, the meaningful statistics column of Table 10 is 'cumulative'. Hence, whilst the mode is a meaningful statistic for data defined on the ratio scale, neither the geometric mean nor the coefficient of variation are meaningful statistics for data defined on the nominal, ordinal or interval scales.

Table 10 The Stevens scales of measurement

Scale	Basic operations	Group structure (J)	Meaningful statistics
Nominal	Determination of equality	Permutation group (any one-to-one substitution)	Number of cases Mode Contingency correlation
Ordinal	Determination of greater or less than	Order preserving group (any monotonic increasing function)	Median Percentiles Rank order correlation
Interval	Determination of equality of intervals or differences	General linear group ($y = a + bx$)	Average Variance Product moment correlation
Ratio	Determination of equality of ratios	Similarity group ($y = bx$)	Geometric mean Coefficient of variation Ratios of two measurements

Case studies

Freddy and the average student

Freddy is a conscientious lecturer who thinks carefully about the grades he allocates to the students under his charge. He has two tutorial classes in his hamburgerology course; the first is predominantly made up of extremely bright students, although there are a few not-so-bright students as well, whilst the second tutorial is composed only of 'average' students. In the most recent examination set by Freddy the first tutorial returned a much higher average mark than the second tutorial and, as Freddy expected, the dispersion of marks as measured by the standard deviation was higher for the first as compared to the second tutorial. Unfortunately, Freddy made the mistake of setting an examination which was far too difficult and the university authorities have asked him to 'scale' the examination marks so that a higher proportion of students obtain a mark in excess of 50%. Freddy does so but now finds that the first tutorial returns both an average mark and a standard deviation of marks which is lower than those for the second tutorial. Freddy is perplexed by this until the university's Registrar points out that his students' examination marks are defined on the ordinal scale. Since neither the average nor the standard deviation are meaningful statistics when applied to data defined on the ordinal scale, it is not surprising Freddy should find that results obtained using one measurement rule are 'reversed' when he uses an alternative rule.

Linda finds the difference

Linda is writing a thesis about the differences between male and female employees in a multinational company. She has obtained information about their level of educational achievement, which she defines as leaving full-time education after completing GCSEs, A-levels, first degree, Master's degree and a PhD, and codes these as 1, 2, 3, 4 and 5 respectively. Linda tests the difference in the educational achievement between male and female employees using a t-test. Her supervisor points out that the t-test may be applied only to data that is measured on an interval or ratio scale, and that the educational achievement variable is measured on an ordinal scale. The supervisor points out that the appropriate test to assess the difference between the educational achievement of males and females is the Mann-Whitney test.

James learns from his mistake

James was analysing data concerning the officer rank and tenure in months of soldiers. He gave the analysis to his supervisor to review. The supervisor found that James had assessed the relationship between rank and tenure by calculating the product moment correlation coefficient between them. The supervisor recognised that this is an inappropriate statistical test because the product moment correlation coefficient can be applied only to data measured on an interval or ratio scale. The soldiers' rank is ordinal scaled data, and the appropriate test to apply is the Spearman's rank correlation coefficient. When James' supervisor tells James that the statistical analysis was incorrect James was disappointed, but determined to carry out the statistical analysis correctly.

Discussion points

1. Why is it important to ensure that the appropriate statistical test is applied to data?

2. Which statistical tests are the most appropriate for analysing nominal, ordinal, interval and ratio scaled data?

3. What are the implications of applying an inappropriate statistical test to nominal, ordinal, interval and ratio scaled data?

Questions and answers

Q. *I have obtained information about the grades of students in a test. The grades are 5, 4, 3, 2 and 1, with 5 representing the highest grade and 1 representing the lowest grade. Which statistical tests can I apply to this data?*

A. This is ordinal scaled data because the grades assigned to the test results indicate that there is a relationship between the grades. Namely, 5 is the higher grade than 4, 3, 2 and 1, 4 is a higher grade than 3, 2, and 1 etc., but there is no indication of the size of the interval between grades. The only statistical tests that may be applied to this data are those appropriate for nominal and ordinal scaled data. These include the mode and median. The mean cannot be used because this statistical test is permissible only when there is at least interval scaled data.

Q. *I have been given some data about the country of origin of students. How should I analyse this data?*

A. This data is recorded on a nominal measurement scale. This scale is used to classify objects into particular categories. In this case students are classified into their country of origin. The coding used to classify the various countries may be changed without altering the basic information provided. The only permissible statistical tests are those which are unaffected by any changes in the coding of data, such as the mode and frequency counts.

Q. *I want to assess the correlation between the height in centimetres and weight in kilograms of a group of students. What is the most appropriate statistical test?*

A. As both height and weight are measured using a ratio scale the most appropriate statistical test for assessing the correlation between them is the product moment correlation. This should be used in preference to the rank order correlation which is a less powerful statistical test that should be applied when at least one of the scales of measurement is an ordinal scale.

Getting Down to Brass Tacks:
The Hard Graft of Writing
Norma Green

One-minute summary – The deadline is looming but it is not easy to commit thought and findings to hard copy. Overcoming the writer's block and producing a product for which you can be rightly proud takes time and effort. However, there are steps and processes which can ease the pain and smooth the rough places. In this chapter you will find help under the following headings:

▶ preparing for writing
▶ mobilising the parallel skills
▶ engaging in the writing process
▶ adjusting the nuts and bolts.

Preparing for writing

Writing is more than a mechanical process. It is not only a revelation of what you have learnt, discovered, or worked out, but it is a statement of your beliefs and by your style – a portrayal of yourself. The commitment of ideas to the written word requires determination.

What is necessary to prepare for writing?
▶ mental readiness
▶ physical necessities.

How can I be mentally ready to write?
A lot of reading and thinking to clarify your purpose and goals needs to precede writing. You have been immersed in the detail of your subject. You need to step back and survey from a distance what you have gleaned, with a critical eye for prioritisation. You must convey concisely and accurately what you consider to be the kernels of your investigation. You may have written your thesis statement a long time ago. Perhaps it needs adjusting now. Your attitude needs to be positive and your confidence firm.

You may have a procrastinating nature. Allow yourself the activities of procrastination and you will probably speed your passage through it toward being able to get started. You need to be *ready* to write, so unfinished business, pressing priorities, personal rituals all need to be dealt with to clear your mind to face the task of writing. Fear of the commitment required by the writing process feeds procrastination. You need to take courage. Your writing will be more satisfactory if you make this necessary mental journey.

Hall (1994) has identified three stages of writer's block, any one of which may occur during the writing process. You may find you can not begin *to work at all*; or you may be unable to begin *to write*; or you may be unable *to finish* what you have begun. The key to solving these difficulties is to identify them, then deal with the root problem.

What do I need to do to be physically prepared?

It's easy to overlook the importance of the obvious requirements, but if you don't make provision, you will find the writing process more tedious and less inspired. You need to:

▶ Identify your time of day for optimum production.
▶ Organise your references, notes, and necessary equipment for writing.
▶ Provide space, light, comfortable temperature, and refreshments.
▶ Choose a comfortable place (or places) to work where you feel productive and won't be distracted.

Most people have an optimum time for productive work. If you are not a morning person, don't force yourself into the early bird mode. Work regularly at your best times. Take breaks. Eat regularly and take exercise. Establish and maintain a routine.

Choose a comfortable, convenient place to work (or, if you thrive on variety, have more than one place) where the conditions are conducive to productive work. Organise yourself so that everything you need is to hand. Keep it together. Tidy up after each session. Write yourself a note about what you want to do next so that when you start again, you don't start cold.

Mobilising parallel skills

The success of the finished thesis depends not only on the ability of the researcher to undertake research and write clearly, but also on the candidate's skill in:

▶ searching
▶ reading
▶ note-taking
▶ record-keeping.

Searching for relevant material

Beginning a search does not need to be random or aimless. Begin with the bibliography of the definitive text; use reading lists produced by your supervisor or lecturers; or leads from discussions with colleagues. Becoming efficient in the use of OPACS *Libertas* binary word search of your own library catalogue or through JANET in other academic libraries and/or databases, such as BIDS/ISI, Web of Knowledge and OCLC FirstSearch is essential. Since the Internet carries so much up-to-date information, you should be sure to bookmark sites and download documents in order to make the best use of your time. Web search engines are invaluable. (Check the glossary for any unfamiliar terms.)

Reading actively and critically

In order to discover the context of your research, active critical reading must take place. Employing an appropriate speed of reading develops your strategy of attack on the volume of material you have to handle. You may *skim, scan* or *study read* as explained in Figure 12.

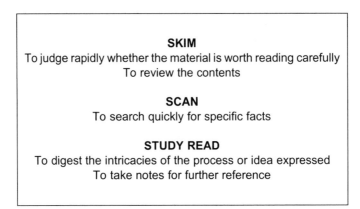

Figure 12. Active and critical reading strategies.

Whatever strategy you employ, the most effective way to read is *actively*. Figure 13 sets out the process you need to follow to do this. It is essential that you read *critically*, as shown in Figure 14.

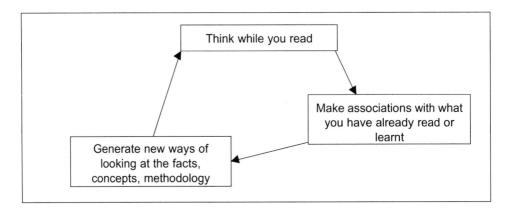

Figure 13. How to read actively.

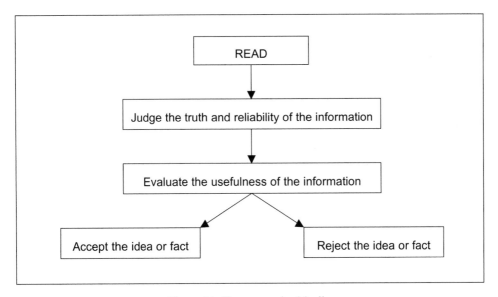

Figure 14. How to read critically.

Record keeping to save valuable time

The one activity that can wreck your timetable is the preparation of the bibliography. You can be chasing illusive references you are sure you read somewhere ages ago to get complete bibliographic data, unless you make a firm rule to write a file card for every book, article, unpublished paper you ever touch from the very beginning of your work. You may prefer to keep the data on a floppy disk, but you will save yourself valuable time and endless frustration by writing down in some consistent format all the essentials as soon as you touch any source. Make value judgements of the contents. If the reference is useless to you, or appears that way at the time you first look at it, you should make a note to that effect, so that you don't waste time in double handling. You may like to date when you first handled the reference. A note detailing the scope of the reference is also helpful. If you alphabetise your sources, you are a long way toward finalising your bibliography. Figures 15 and 16 suggest a format you may wish to adopt for file cards.

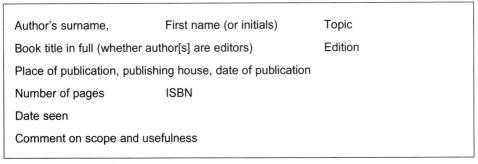

Figure 15. Sample bibliographic card entry for a book.

Author's surname, first name (or initials)	Topic
Title in full, name of the journal, volume number, Issue number	
Date of publication	
Number of pages	
Date seen	
Comment on scope and usefulness	

Figure 16. Sample bibliographic card entry for a journal.

Plagiarism is academic theft. Read the University regulations on plagiarism to be very clear how you need to acknowledge someone else's work exactly. Put the author's name, an identifying title and the page number where you keep your notes of sources read, and you will be less likely to fail to acknowledge your source.

Engaging in the writing process

Some supervisors will ask candidates to prepare a literature review following reading around the subject. Others may ask for background information which will form at least part of the introduction to the thesis. Still others may suggest that you begin writing up your materials and methods section first. Whatever you begin writing, you need to gather your thoughts before you start. The writing process, which is summarised for you in Figure 17, includes:

▶ brainstorming
▶ prioritising and planning
▶ drafting
▶ observing academic writing conventions
▶ redrafting.

Brainstorming and organising ideas

Brainstorming should follow after reading, which provides the grist for the exercise. Trite as it may sound, a session of allowing your mind the freedom of ranging unleashed around the concepts of your topic will produce a large share of the central considerations, relationships and interrelationships around which to build your thesis. Set yourself a time limit in a quiet place and write notes at random without making any judgement of anything you are writing.

Once these points are on paper, the process of evaluating their relevance and ordering them can begin. However, you may prefer to *Mind Map* (Buzan, 1988) or produce a spidergram in your brainstorm session rather than working out the relationships after brainstorming. If so, you might like to use *Inspiration* software which provides a way of mind mapping on the computer. The important point is to engage in unfettered thought in order not only to draw out the essential elements of the topic but to envision new relationships among the concepts. You then have plenty of material to draw from when you go dry.

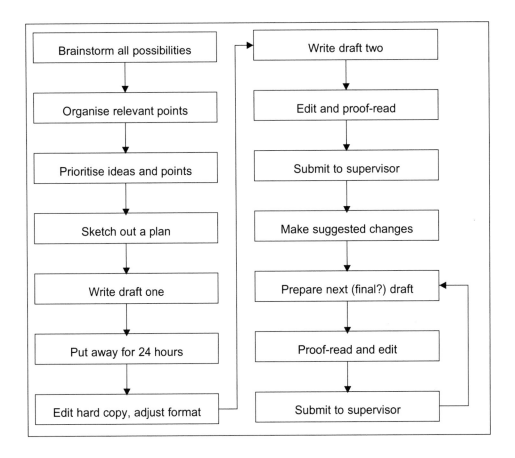

Figure 17. The writing process.

Prioritising and planning

Once the brainstorm has produced a battery of ideas, you ought to analyse the results for links between concepts, facts, elements, facets, and ideas. You need to be ruthless in selecting and prioritising the points, discarding irrelevant points, and setting aside any whose value is uncertain. This planning stage is central to your work because the longer you labour on an extended piece of writing the less focused you become about the whole. If you have taken time initially to isolate all the significant ideas and lay out an ordered consistent plan, then you are less likely to become bogged down in details which may be irrelevant to the development of the thesis. The actual format of your plan is individual (not necessarily the format you learned at school!). However, if you follow the hierarchy of your department house style, you will have an easier time complying with presentation regulations.

Drafting the first time

Writing is a building process. Paragraph should build on paragraph expanding, exploring and arguing the case. Ideas should follow a clear sequence to take the reader with you. The first paragraph needs to be in the present tense to establish the scope, suggest the parameters and their limits, and introduce definitions germane to the thesis. The microcosm of the paragraph is explained in Figure 18, which you can use as a template for writing a paragraph.

Observing academic writing conventions

Paying careful attention to your writing style aids the reader's understanding of your point of view, the details of your research, your analysis and your conclusions. You should aim for:

▶ cohesion
▶ clarity
▶ conciseness
▶ impersonal style
▶ consistency.

I. General statement about the topic
Focus on the important distinguishing characteristics you want to emphasise
Probably one sentence

II. Expansion of the main points
Say something more about each part of the general statement using the same order.
Perhaps 2 or 3 sentences
(At this point, you could write a whole paragraph about each aspect, and put examples within each paragraph for each aspect.)

III. Examples about aspects of the topic
Choose one or more of these types of examples:
Quotations (properly cited)
Examples of important aspects
Examples of unusual aspects which strengthen your point of view
Maybe up to 5 sentences

IV Summary and concluding statement
Draw together the main ideas by briefly mentioning each and suggesting where you have reached at this point
Hint: include something that provides a bridge to the next aspect
Probably 2 or 3 sentences

Figure 18. How a paragraph should be written.

Cohesion is essential
The orderly progression of subsections, sections, and chapters following a well conceived outline will show logical development of the content. Cohesion can be achieved by the use of *parallel construction* for ideas of equal importance, similar functions, or similar constituents; *transition words* to introduce a sentence, to link ideas within the sentence, or show relationships within the paragraph; or *subordination* showing the relative importance of ideas or parts of ideas. Practices which can destroy cohesion include:

▶ generalities and vague references using indefinite pronouns, e.g., *many, some, a lot, they*

▶ repetitive sentence construction, e.g., *always using one type of sentence, or joining ideas with 'and'*

▶ red herrings, e.g., *misplaced, irrelevant or unnecessary ideas.*

Clarity aids understanding
Precise, well balanced sentences should use complex sentence construction to show ideas in relation to each other. Concrete terminology conveys clear meaning. Practices which can destroy clarity are:

▶ a profusion of simple sentences
▶ overuse of expressions like 'etc'.
▶ oversimplification
▶ misuse of jargon (technical language).

Conciseness sharpens the point
Closely related to clarity is conciseness because clarity is aided by an economy of carefully chosen words, the essence of conciseness. Use a thesaurus in conjunction with a dictionary to choose the most appropriate word. Enemies of conciseness are:

▶ slang and colloquial expressions, i.e., *any words which are essentially spoken language*

▶ superfluous expressions which provide padding to the text, e.g., *Let us now turn to..., It is significant to note the fact that...*

▶ pretentious, flowery language or stilted pompous old-fashioned civil service style

▶ pedantic inclusion of minute detail

▶ words which are too general, e.g., *good, well, high, big.*

Impersonal style raises the register
Most disciplines encourage students to adopt an impersonal style so that the focus

is on the research rather than on the researcher. To achieve an impersonal style, avoid:

▶ the use of *I, we, you*

▶ exclamation marks

▶ underlining words in a conversational way for emphasis

▶ using a dash instead of a conjunction (*and, but, for*), a comma or a semi-colon

▶ phrasal verbs, e.g., *went up, thought well of*

▶ contractions, e.g., *it's, doesn't, won't.*

Consistency provides order
The overriding component is consistency because it sets the limits for all the conventions mentioned above. It is essential to establish a format which extends throughout since this is a tacit way of guiding the reader through the text. Therefore, headings, indentations, foot or end note format, bibliographic content and format, inclusion of examples, and lists, all need to be uniform in their presentation.

Redrafting
When your first draft is finished, put it away for 24 hours. You return to it with fresh eyes to see it more objectively, therefore, you are better able to see what changes you need to make. Don't be afraid to revise, but don't overdo it. Research shows that you can alter your initial intention if you redraft too many times.

Hand your edited, proof-read draft to your supervisor for advice on the content. (Editing and proof-reading operations are discussed separately below.) You may be advised to reorder or add material, to adjust your style, format and grammar. When you have discussed the changes or additions which are needed, begin to redraft those sections. Remember that the changes you make may affect other parts of the already written text. You must edit those sections, too. Don't be discouraged; it is in your interest to make your thesis as nearly perfect as you can. Many supervisors do not have the time available to see a thesis more than once. The onus of responsibility is on you to present an acceptable piece of work. When you are satisfied with your revised draft, submit it to your supervisor as ready for examination.

Adjusting the nuts and bolts

The final adjustments to your script are the activities which will help to ensure that you are delivering a quality product.

▶ controlling your verbs
▶ citing with care
▶ editing with judgement
▶ proof-reading with precision.

Controlling your verbs
Verbs cause problems unless you control your use of three aspects:

▶ Choose *present* or *past tense* as your main tense; keep to those unless meaning demands a change.
▶ Make sure that verbs agree in number and person with the subjects.
▶ Make appropriate choice of mood: *active* or *passive*.

Choosing tenses
The present tense allows you to state principles, definitions, and accepted facts. Where an historical perspective is necessary, the past tense should be used. More complex tenses can be used where the subject matter demands.

Making agreement
Agreement means that the subject and verb are both in the same form. If a subject is plural, then the verb must be plural. Similarly, if one is singular, the other must be singular. There are some problem words and phrases like: *government, each, either, one of the samples*, which are singular; whereas, *data, people, all, both...and...*, are plural.

Choosing a mood
In English verbs are either *active* or *passive*; that is, their subjects are either *doing the action* or *receiving it*. The passive puts the emphasis on the person or thing receiving the action rather than on the one performing it. A verb in a passive sentence is always a *verb phrase* that has:

1.   a form of the verb *to be*, and
2.   the *past participle of the main verb*.

The *active* is the most commonly used mood, but the *passive* is useful for thesis writing when:

▶ The subject is unknown, common knowledge, or unnecessary.

▶ The subject and the object need to be reversed for emphasis.

▶ An awkward referent needs to be avoided. (To be sure what is being referred to.)

▶ The use of *I, we, you, this, there* ought to be avoided.

▶ Variety of expression is desirable.

The passive is handy, but *don't overuse it* or the text will be limp.

Citing with care

Each institution (sometimes, each department) has its own preferred style of citing references. The established guides are Kate Turabian or John Spink who have made the Chicago Manual of Style accessible, the Harvard style used by The Open University, and a third is the MLA Stylesheet. Citing documents from the Internet is also necessary. A Web page which gives extensive advice on how to cite material from the Internet is: *http://www.bournemouth.ac.uk/library/using/guide_to_citing_internet-source.html*. Citations need to be both in the text where the actual quotation is located, and a full citation in the bibliography. Refer to the section above about bibliographic cards for the information required in a full citation. Citing is meticulous work. The important thing to remember is to choose a style and follow it consistently.

Editing with judgement

Editing precedes proof-reading. When editing, you must read each sentence critically to see that it says what you mean it to say. Words and phrases must be in the correct order to convey the precise meaning you intend, avoiding ambiguity. You must see that the sentences are complete ideas which are moving the argument or revelation of the situation forward without contradictions. Paragraphs need to be in a logical order. Tables, charts, graphs must appear near the text to which they refer. Irrelevant statements, poor choice of words and unnecessary examples need to be removed. Missing evidence needs to be added. Parallel constructions should occur where necessary. Punctuation should be appropriate to help convey accurate meaning. Check that the sequence of headings is correct, reflects what is in the text, and makes sense. The conclusion must be a true representative of what has been said. Editing is a thinking activity in which you are judging what is written objectively.

Proof-reading with precision

The final activity is proof-reading which involves *mechanically reading words*, not ideas, looking for all the possible typographical errors, misspellings, forgotten punctuation and/or capital letters, noun and verb plurals, formatting, spacing, numbering, widows and orphans. Don't forget that the spellchecker allows some howlers. You are not reading for sense, meaning or ideas when you are proof-reading; you are reading to catch mechanical errors. It is wise to proof-read for formatting errors in a reading separate from one looking for errors in English.

Case studies

Adrian misses the point

Adrian was well motivated, made progress in the initial stages and was finished well before the deadline. He was very satisfied with his product, feeling as proud as a peacock. As soon as his supervisor started reading the draft, he realised that he would have to approach the candidate forthrightly. The long complex sentences with obscure synonyms dredged out of a thesaurus without reference to a dictionary, lumbered on. Evidence of plagiarism stood out in the abrupt changes in style. When Adrian called to see his supervisor to collect his accolades, the mentor drew his attention to the shortcomings and changes necessary. Adrian, affronted by the suggestion of changes, became very defensive; after all, it was his research. The supervisor had anticipated the likelihood of an altercation because Adrian had sought minimal guidance from the outset. In the end, a lengthy extension was necessary to allow Adrian time to rewrite.

Janet finds a way

Janet sat surrounded by open books, photocopied journal articles, post-it notes with reminders of other possible references, heaps of dog-eared A4 sheets of notes and downloaded documents from the Web. Meticulous planning had been done. Janet had spent days producing sheaves of outlines trying to ensure that all previous work on the topic was included. Propelled by the urge to get on with the job and not waste time, Janet began to write. She soon realised that she had too much text. She began to cross out sections, editing ruthlessly. Before long, she realised that the changes had blurred the accuracy of the sense initially intended. She was very discouraged by the enormity of the task. A friend suggested that she go back to her notes to colour-code the points following her outlined plan. Janet found that this procedure rescued her from wallowing in detail, helping her to focus on essentials. Her next draft was much improved.

Sian breaks out

Sian is a classic procrastinator. She is so busy with outside activities and in the business of living, that she never gets to the library until an hour before closing time. Becoming aware that time was passing, Sian took hold of herself to try to curtail her delaying tactics. Changing her lifestyle, she amassed a body of respectable notes and a meticulous bibliography. She sat down for a brainstorm session and was able to Mind Map the main focus. The discipline she was imposing on herself made her tense, but she could see results. She decided to write directly onto the word processor from her mind maps. The freedom to add, move, or delete text aided her creativity. At the end of each writing session, she took a hard copy to proof-read. When she finished a chapter, she edited it in the light of the whole. Sian's progress was steady; her supervisor was satisfied; she finished on time and gained a distinction for her thesis.

Discussion points

1. How important is it to begin to write early in the Master's degree programme?

2. What can be gained from reading books and articles about my topic? I have done the research, and I know all there is to know about the subject firsthand.

3.   Does everyone attack writing in the same way? Is there one right way?

Questions and answers

Q. *I finished my literature review four months ago. My supervisor keeps referring me to newly published journal articles. What should I do?*

A.   You need to discuss the most appropriate cut-off point for the inclusion of newly published material with your supervisor. If the articles significantly alter your conclusions, you should certainly include them. However, be sure that you redraft every point that is affected by the new findings in order to maintain consistency. It is important to keep up to date, but you may need to weigh up the amount of time which will be required to make all the changes necessary against the sagacity of omitting them.

Q. *How important is it for me to write good grammatical English?*

A.   In order to express the subtleties of your ideas and your findings, you need to be able to show those relationships through the construction of your sentences as well as by the careful choice of vocabulary. Conversational English does not carry the weight of the meaning you need to express. From your reading, you will gain a feeling for the register you need to adopt. You might like a grammar book handy for reference; but you don't need to spend your time reading it from cover to cover.

Q. *What are the sections of a thesis?*

A.   As might be expected, a scientific thesis and an arts thesis differ in format. The sections which you should expect to have are shown in Figure 19. There are some official pages required at the beginning including a declaration and statements. You will have a title page, maybe a dedication, acknowledgements, and a table of contents, lists of tables and figures.

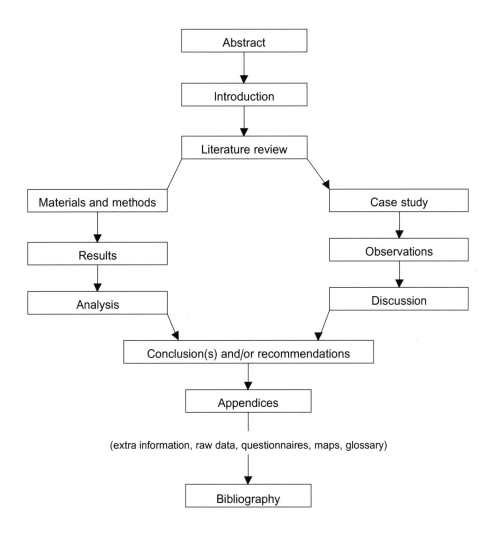

Figure 19. The sections of a thesis.

Legal and Ethical Issues
Allison Coleman and John Williams

One-minute summary – The aim of this chapter is to enable a student doing research and writing a thesis to use the works of others without breach of copyright or confidentiality laws, and to protect his or her own work against improper use by others.

Students will want to photocopy materials, to quote from the works of others or to use their maps and diagrams in their thesis or any subsequent publications. They may search the Internet and electronic databases and download materials, and they may want to share software. They may carry out questionnaire surveys or interview people. Each of these activities raises copyright and/or confidentiality problems.

In this chapter you will find information and advice on how to deal with these issues under the following headings:

▶ sources of copyright law
▶ what rights does copyright confer?
▶ the issue of confidentiality.

Sources of copyright law

Before starting – a warning! The law of copyright is complex; it is riddled with exceptions, and changes with both the date and the type of work. This chapter is too short to do anything other than highlight issues; so, if you think you have a copyright problem you should consult an expert. There is a further reading list at the end of this chapter listing specialist works on copyright which may be of value to you.

The most recent Act of Parliament is the Copyright, Designs and Patents Act 1988 (the 1988 Act), which governs works created after 1st August 1989. However, previous Copyright Acts are still important and may apply to works created before that date. Also, the 1988 Act applies only to the UK. The laws of other countries may well be different.

What rights does copyright confer?

Copyright confers two main sets of rights: economic rights and moral rights. Economic rights enable a copyright owner to earn money. They are the exclusive rights to carry out activities indicated in Figure 20.

> ▶ copy the work
>
> ▶ rent or lend the work
>
> ▶ issue copies to the public (to distribute it)
>
> ▶ perform, play or show the work in public
>
> ▶ to broadcast it or include it in a cable programme
>
> ▶ make an adaptation of it (e.g. to translate it) or to do any of the above with an adaptation.

Figure 20. Economic rights conferred by copyright.

Because the rights are exclusive to the owner of copyright, he or she is the only person entitled to do any of the acts listed above; others need the consent of the copyright owner and consent can be conditional on the payment of a fee. The law is fully up to date and covers doing any of the above by traditional methods or electronically. However, there are a number of very important exceptions to the 1988 Act, known as permitted acts. The one most frequently relied on by academic researchers and students is fair dealing for the purposes of research or private study. This legitimises photocopying or downloading of a certain proportion of certain types of copyright work. By way of contrast, when you are writing your thesis or publishing an article you will rely mainly on another exception, that relating to criticism and review. Infringements of copyright and permitted acts are considered further below.

The author of a work also has moral rights as indicated in Figure 21.

> ▶ the right to be identified as the author or director of a work
>
> ▶ the right to object to derogatory treatment
>
> ▶ the right to object to false attribution of a work
>
> ▶ the right to privacy of certain films and photographs.

Figure 21. Moral rights conferred by copyright.

Moral rights have become particularly useful to authors whose works are published electronically, then reproduced in whole or in part without being correctly attributed, or which have been copied from a database or the Internet, then published in an altered form.

One important limitation on copyright is that it protects only the way in which material is set out, that is its expression; it does not protect the underlying idea. So long as a work is not actually copied, either wholly or substantially, lifting the underlying idea and expressing it in a different way amounts only to plagiarism. Plagiarism is a transgression of academic good practice and if committed by students may breach disciplinary rules but it does not necessarily involve breach of copyright. Plagiarism can be avoided by adequate footnoting or citation and should not be ignored – each university will have a statement on plagiarism and you should find out what yours has to say on the matter.

What do copyright laws protect?

Copyright law protects nine main categories of items, known as 'works'. These are:

- ▶ original literary, dramatic, musical or artistic works
- ▶ sound recordings, films, broadcasts or cable programmes
- ▶ the typographical arrangement of published editions.

Many of these categories are, however, subdivided. Literary works, for instance, covers not only books and articles, but also 'a table or compilation and ... a computer program', and artistic work covers, amongst other things, photographs, diagrams and maps. Databases are also protected by copyright.

Who owns copyright?

The first owner of copyright in a work is its author, i.e., the person who first creates it, but there are also special rules for joint authorship and for works created by employees in the course of their employment. Copyright may be transferred to another by written assignment, and it passes by will or intestacy on death. Authors may agree to transfer copyright in their work to their publishers under the publishing contract. In these circumstances, publishers become the owners of copyright. Publishers are therefore commonly the owners of copyright in books and articles. Copyright licences are also common, particularly with software. Here the owner retains copyright, but the licensee is given a right to use the software subject to the terms of the licence. This right to use software does not normally authorise giving it to others or allowing them to use it. They should 'buy' their own.

How long does copyright last?

Under the Copyright, Designs and Patents Act 1988 copyright in literary, dramatic, musical and artistic works lasted for the life of the author, plus fifty years. Since 1st January 1996, the copyright term for most of these works has been extended by the Duration of Copyright Regulations 1995 (the 1995 Regulations) to life plus seventy years. This means that many works, which had dropped out of copyright, are now once again protected by what is known as 'revived copyright'. The 1995 Regulations are exceptionally complicated and are generally beyond the scope of this chapter. A useful account can be found in Flint *et al.* (2000).

Infringement of copyright

There are two types of infringement or breach of copyright: primary and secondary. Firstly, primary infringement: as stated above, the owner of copyright has the exclusive right to copy the work; to rent or to lend it; to issue copies to the public; to perform or show the work in public; to broadcast or include it in a cable programme or to make an adaptation of it. If anyone else does any of these acts without permission, it will amount to primary infringement of copyright. This type of infringement involves breach only of the civil rights of the copyright owner, and it can be committed innocently, i.e., there is no need for the infringer to know that the work is protected by copyright, or that the act constitutes infringement. Primary infringement is not a criminal offence (compare this to secondary infringement described below).

The whole work need not be copied, performed etc. for it to amount to a breach of copyright. It is sufficient if a substantial part is used without consent. Copying a section of a work can therefore breach copyright. The test as to whether a part of a work is substantial is not just related to the quantity of what is taken, but also takes into account its quality – is it an important part, or key component, or a clearly recognisable part? If it is qualitatively important, it does not matter that the part taken is in fact quite small in relation to the work as a whole. To some extent the courts work on the principle that if it is worth taking it must be important and is worth protecting by copyright. This means that the copier has to be very careful. The normal remedies for infringement of the civil rights of a copyright owner are an injunction to prevent further breach of the law, or damages for a breach which has already occurred. It should, however, be noted that certain acts will not amount to infringement of copyright. These exceptions are discussed below under the heading of permitted acts. Read this section before you panic about photocopying or downloading!

Secondary infringement of copyright breaches the civil rights of the copyright owner, but is also a criminal offence. Basically it involves dealing in copyright works. However, in order to be liable the infringer must have a 'guilty mind', i.e., must know or have reason to believe that there is a breach of copyright.

Permitted acts

Researchers rely heavily on one particular exception to copyright protection. This is 'fair dealing for the purposes of research or private study' and it enables students and researchers to copy (e.g. photocopy or download) a proportion of a literary, dramatic, musical or artistic work (but note, not the other works such as sound recordings) without infringing copyright in it, or, in the case of a published edition, without infringing copyright in the typographical arrangement (which belongs to the publisher).

The governing principle in this particular provision is that the copying must be fair. In America it is known as the fair use provision, a description which is arguably better than our notion of fair dealing. If the copying is of a large proportion of a work (or a whole work e.g. a whole book) which is in print and available in the bookshops, the use will invariably be unfair and the copying will breach copyright.

Assessing fairness can obviously be quite difficult. Publishers have reached agreements called licensing agreements with universities and others which set out what in their view is fair use. Persons who copy within these guidelines will not be sued for infringement of copyright. The terms of these licensing agreements are found in summary form alongside most photocopying machines. Read them and abide by them.

Authors in their writings make frequent reference to the works of others. If the ideas of another are used, but not the expression of the other, there can be no breach of copyright, for, as we saw above, copyright protects the form in which a work is set out and not the underlying ideas as such. The other author should be cited to avoid allegations of plagiarism, rather than breach of copyright laws.

If an author wishes to quote from the work of another, or use maps, drawings or tables of another, copyright may be infringed unless the act is permitted under another heading, namely, fair dealing for the purposes of criticism or review. The criticism or review may be of the work itself, or of a performance of it, and in both cases it must be accompanied by a sufficient acknowledgement. Again the governing principle is that the use (or dealing) must be fair. It is dangerous to quote large chunks of the work of others. It also does not impress the examiner. 'Sufficient acknowledgement' means that the source must be cited in full.

Following full bibliographic citation standard practice should avoid problems. Help is provided on this in Chapter 5 and your supervisor should be able to advise you.

Various other acts are permitted by the 1988 Act, but they relate mainly to copying by libraries and for the purposes of educational instruction and are not covered here. They will apply to you only if, in addition to research, you also teach.

The issue of confidentiality

Confidentiality is something that we often take for granted. When we go to the doctor we do not expect the content of our 'confidential' consultation to be public knowledge. We are entitled to rely on the doctor's duty of confidentiality. Of course we can tell others the details of our discussions because the confidentiality belongs to us – but the doctor is prevented from doing so. Much of the law of confidentiality has been developed in relation to the doctor/patient relationship. However, the law extends much further and may embrace some of the research activity undertaken by students.

There are aspects of research, which involve the researcher obtaining from another person information that may be of a confidential nature. The most obvious example of this is when you compile a questionnaire that you then ask members of the public to complete. Some may simply involve the interviewee ticking a series of boxes. Others may require a free text answer to be given and the researcher may be centrally involved in obtaining the information and recording the views of the interviewee. Usually the name of the interviewee will not be included in the processed data. However, the researcher will often know who the interviewee is and may be privy to sensitive information about their lifestyle, commercially sensitive matters or financial matters. The question arises whether in law such information is subject to a duty of confidence.

The Law of Confidentiality

The House of Lords in the case of the *Attorney General* v *Guardian Newspapers Ltd* (otherwise known as the Spycatcher Case) discussed the law of confidentiality. Lord Goff said that a duty of confidentiality arises in the following circumstances:

1. The information concerned is confidential

2. It comes to the knowledge of a person (the confidant) in circumstances where he or she had notice, or is held to have agreed, that the information is confidential, with the effect that it would be just that he or she should be precluded from disclosing the information

3. It is in the public interest that the confidentiality should be protected.

Clearly information is not confidential when it is already in the public domain. The information may be a matter of public record (for example the performance of a publicly quoted company), or the individual themselves may have previously made it public.

The duty arises in a number of different relationships. Perhaps the most common application of the duty of confidentiality is in the doctor/patient relationship. However, it may also arise out of a contract. This may be of particular interest to research students who are funded by a commercial, public or voluntary undertaking. The agreement may well contain a duty to keep certain types of information confidential. Such a contractual term has important implications for a research student who intends that his or her work will be disseminated as widely as possible. If faced with such a clause it is essential to be clear how extensive any restrictions on publication may be. Do not be afraid to raise this with the body concerned before you actually start your research. Where an issue of confidentiality does arise, most universities have a system whereby a bar on access to a thesis can be granted for reasons of confidentiality – it might be worth finding out about this as it could mean the difference between proceeding or not proceeding with research.

Particular issues need to be addressed when interviewing people. In fairness to those who agree to give up their time to fill in your questionnaire or to be interviewed by you, it is important that there is agreement between you on the issue of confidentiality. Is the interview confidential? Does the person agree to their remarks being attributed to them in your thesis? Can you use the information they provide in your thesis, or do they intend it to be used only as background information? Are there times during the interview when they wish to go 'off the record'? Do they demand the right to 'check the accuracy' of your use of the information provided?

The important principle here is that issues surrounding confidentiality must be resolved prior to the interview taking place. Unless both parties agree at the outset whether or not the interview is confidential, and if so to what extent, problems may arise. You may be of the opinion that the interview is not confidential whereas the interviewee may think the opposite. It is essential that the ground rules be agreed at the outset.

Can legal confidences ever be broken?

As can be seen from the Spycatcher Case the public interest must support the confidentiality. This suggests that there may be situations where the public interest demands that a confidence is broken. Confidentiality is not an absolute principle and the law recognises this. In the case of *W* v *Egdell* the court allowed a doctor to break a doctor/patient confidence. The question was whether a confidential report on the mental health of the patient could be disclosed to the Home Office on the grounds of public safety. The court said it had to balance on the one hand the public interest in maintaining the confidential nature of the doctor/patient relationship, and on the other the public interest in public safety. After considering these competing interests the court came down in favour of disclosure – the public safety argument outweighed the doctor/patient argument. However, this is not always the case. In the case of *X* v *Y* (note the names aren't given here to protect the confidentiality of those involved in the case!) it was decided that the public interest in doctor/patient confidentiality outweighed the public's interest in knowing that two doctors diagnosed as HIV positive were continuing to practise.

Where a confidence can be broken under the principle outlined in *Egdell* it is important that any disclosure is restricted to those who, in pursuit of the public interest, need to know.

Social science researchers may encounter such dilemmas when undertaking interviews. It is possible that a rapport will be built up between the interviewer and the interviewee and the former may become a confidant for the latter. This can create difficult ethical and legal problems, especially if evidence of child abuse or the abuse of a vulnerable adult is disclosed. It is essential in deciding whether a disclosure should be made to consider the public interest dimension. Such decisions should be discussed with your supervisor or some other person (being careful not to identify the confidant during these preliminary discussions). Researchers may also become aware of other forms of criminal activity during their research.

Police access to confidential information

The Police and Criminal Evidence Act 1984 allows the police to have access to certain categories of confidential information, subject to satisfying the safeguards contained in the Act. These provisions are only used in a few cases. Nevertheless it is important not to forget that access may be possible.

Ethical considerations

Although information in your possession may not have been obtained in accordance with the statement of Lord Goff in *Spycatcher*, some thought should be given to the ethics of disclosure. The fact that there is no legal duty of confidentiality does not always make it 'right' to disclose. Researchers should be sensitive to issues such as the privacy of the individual and also the consequences of disclosure to the individual and his or her family. Ethical considerations are just as important as legal ones.

Case studies

Tim gets it all wrong

Tim is working hard on his thesis. He has read widely, photocopied everything he can lay his hands on and downloaded all the materials the Internet and on-line databases can provide. He and his friends are overawed by the huge quantity of materials he has built up.

When Tim starts to write, he finds that he really cannot improve on what other authors have already written, so he decides to cut and paste from their works and to string it all together in narrative form. Working right up until the deadline he doesn't have time to add footnotes to any of the sources he has used. He hands his first chapter to his supervisor. He is horrified to find that after all of his hard work, his supervisor is accusing him of lack of originality, of plagiarism and infringement of copyright.

Bethany bites the dust

Bethany has heard of Tim's problems, but thinks she can pull the wool over her supervisor's eyes by finding an obscure out-of-print book that is not in the library of her home university. The book is so good she feels she cannot improve on its mode of expression or analysis. Bethany copies out most of the (rather small book) and submits it as her thesis. Just to be on the safe side (so she thinks) she includes the book in her bibliography.

Unknown to her, her supervisor is a personal friend of the author, has read the book and recognises it instantly. Bethany finds herself being interviewed by the same Unfair Practice Panel as Tim and she too faces allegations of infringement of copyright.

Good old Tom!

Tom decides to read widely before spending money on photocopying and printing. Each item he reads, he adds to his bibliography and notes its importance for his research. By the time he starts to write, his files are very much thinner than

Tim's, but he knows his subject thoroughly and has developed his own ideas. He draws on the work of others, but explains their views in his own words, using quotations sparingly and footnoting a reference to each book, article etc. he has used when developing a point. Tom's supervisor, who is a little jaded after reading Tim's and Bethany's work, is delighted, and tells Tom that he has a bright future as a researcher.

To tell or not to tell? Sian's dilemma

Sian is working on her PhD on the incidence of poverty in remote rural areas. Part of her research involves visiting people in their own homes and asking them a series of questions relating to their income, housing conditions and health. The nature of the questions, and Sian's ability to put people at their ease, means that many people will divulge very personal information. Sian tells all interviewees that the interview is confidential and that they will not be identifiable in the final report. One such interview takes place with Catrin, a thirty-year-old mother of two young children. She lives with her partner, Aled, who is the father of one of the children. When discussing health, Catrin discloses that on occasions Aled is violent towards her. The last time this occurred, Catrin had to go to the Accident and Emergency unit of the local hospital for treatment. She told the hospital that she had 'fallen down the stairs'. Although the medical staff did not believe her, they felt there was nothing they could do. Sian is horrified by this information and fears for Catrin's safety, and for that of the children. However, she is also aware that she has given an undertaking of confidentiality and that to disclose this information to the police would be a breach of that duty. What should she do? Is it there anything that Sian can do prior to the commencement of the interviews to avoid this kind of ethical dilemma?

Discussion points

1. How can copyright be reconciled with freedom of information?

2. Does copyright give too much protection to the owners of rights at the expense of users of information?

3. To what extent does copyright apply in the digital environment?

4. Is the duty of confidentiality ever absolute?

5. How should you balance the competing public interests in the duty of confidentiality and the need to break the duty in certain circumstances?

6. Would you ever feel able to keep a confidence when you know that a third party may be injured unless you disclose the information?

7. What kind of information should be capable of being protected by the duty of confidentiality?

Questions and answers

Q. *Does copyright apply to everything I use and write?*

A. The safest answer to this question is yes, unless you are using very old materials. Most students other than those researching historical matters can therefore assume that all of the laws discussed in this chapter apply.

Q. *Where can I get advice on copyright?*

A. Many Universities and Institutes of Higher Education have Copyright Officers. Contact your registry for the name of this person. Other sources of advice are Industrial Liaison Offices or Open/Distance Learning Units.

Q. *Can I afford to take risks?*

A. No!

Q. *How should I go about trying to resolve the difficult dilemma of whether or not to break a confidence?*

A. It is crucial that you identify clearly the reasons for your ultimate decision (whether to disclose or to reveal the information). Making a record of your reasoning is sensible. It often helps to discuss the ethical dilemma with somebody else who you can trust (e.g. your supervisor), but remember not to disclose the identity (either directly or indirectly) of the beneficiary of the confidentiality. Ultimately, it is your decision, so be convinced in your own mind that you can defend what you eventually do.

Q. *Can an aggrieved person bring a legal action against me for breach of confidence?*

A. Yes.

Q. *If I decide to break a confidence and can justify it in the public interest, does this mean that the information is now in the public domain and I can use it freely?*

A. No. If you decide to disclose in the public interest, you must only disclose it to those people who need to know the information (e.g. the police or the social services).

7

Understanding Submission and Examination Processes

Gina Preston

One-minute summary – This chapter will explain what is usually involved in submitting a thesis. Actual practice varies widely from one institution to another and the aim of this chapter is to point out questions you need to address and when you might need to address them. It is vital that you find out what the exact situation is for you at your university.

The chapter covers the following issues:

▶ submitting your thesis – when should it be submitted, in what format and to whom?
▶ assessing the thesis – who assesses it? possible outcomes
▶ post assessment issues – what happens if you fail?

Submitting your thesis

Thoughts of submitting your thesis are not likely to be at the forefront of your mind until you approach the end of your research or even of your writing up. It is important, however, that you do spend some time fairly early on sorting out what you have to do and when you need to do it. This will help you to establish a schedule that you can stick to and ensure that you are not rushing around at the last moment tying up loose administrative ends when you may desperately need those extra few days to finalise the thesis itself.

Many institutions have very clear rules and a thesis submitted at the wrong time, or in the wrong format will simply not be considered, no matter how wonderful a piece of research it is.

Figure 22 is a flow chart illustrating the questions you need to find answers to before you should start writing your thesis. These questions will be considered in turn now.

Finding the submission procedures

If you are at a university which puts the needs of its students as a priority and has a commitment to the provision of quality information, you should have been provided with a helpful booklet or handout at the beginning of your course which explains the submission procedure. Such booklets are becoming more widely available. Alternatively, your institution may hold induction sessions which explain what you should do. If your institution provides neither of these, ask why not.

If there is no booklet or induction session, you will have to find out the answers to these questions yourself. Try your supervisor to start with. Find out who the key people are in your university administration, get hold of a copy of the university regulations. These will be less easy to read but the information will be there.

Whether you are given a booklet or not, it will be helpful for you to look at what others have done. Go to the library and take a look at theses which have been written recently in your subject area, and at the format and style. Be wary of following this approach without checking that regulations have not changed.

When can I submit?

All institutions have time limits for submission of theses. In general, most full-time Master's courses are of between 12 and 24 months duration, the first 9 or 12 months of which will be the taught element, with a further 3–15 months for writing the thesis.

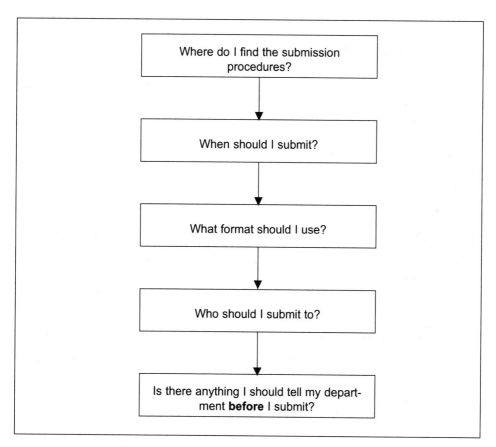

Figure 22. Questions you should find the answers to.

You should have been informed of the exact timetable for your particular course either when you were offered a place or during the first few sessions. If for whatever reason, this is not the case, you should find out now. If you miss the deadline for submission, an excuse that someone told you the wrong information is not likely to be taken seriously. It is your job to ensure you know what is required.

In what format should my thesis be submitted?
Universities vary significantly in their strictness over the presentation of the thesis and indeed in such fundamental issues as word length. In some instances, different departments within an institution have requirements that differ to some extent. Three key questions will be examined here.

1. How long can/should the thesis be?
Word limits vary widely both between institutions and even within institutions themselves. If your thesis is in an arts or humanities subject, you can usually expect the word length to be longer, science subjects often involve a significant practical project, e.g. computer program, and fewer actual words.

   You would usually expect to find a limit of between 10,000 and 20,000 words, although in some cases it could be as few as 4,000 or as many as 50,000. Bear in mind that maximum word lengths are usually what are given and your supervisor should be able to advise you what would be appropriate for your particular project.

2. How should the thesis look?
Many universities will have clearly laid out regulations telling you some or all of the following:

▶ type of paper you should use
▶ typeface
▶ font size
▶ margins

▶ line spacing
▶ how to caption figures and tables.

In all cases it will be expected that the thesis is typewritten or word processed. If you are having your thesis word-processed for you, or if you are doing it yourself, ensure that you follow these regulations from the beginning. It is much harder to go back and reformat it at the end.

3. How should the thesis be presented?
Generally it will be expected that your thesis is presented in soft binding. At some institutions you will be expected to arrange this yourself, at others it may be done for you. In addition, you will have to ensure that you follow the institution house style with regard to:

▶ title page
▶ contents
▶ references
▶ footnotes
▶ page numbering
▶ division into chapters
▶ glossaries
▶ summaries and abstracts
▶ number of copies to submit.

To whom should I submit my thesis?
In many cases the thesis can be submitted in the first instance to either:

▶ your supervisor
▶ course director
▶ course administrator.

Do check, particularly if you intend to post your thesis to a named person, that they are the right person and that they will be around at the time.

You will also need to know what administrative forms need to be submitted with the thesis. Usually you will need to present a summary of approximately 300 words and complete a presentation form in which you sign a declaration supported by your supervisor which states to what degree the research is your own work and that the work has not been submitted for any other degree. Your university is also likely to require proof that you have paid all your fees and you may need to obtain a statement from the finance office to that effect.

It is vital that you complete all the required forms and submit them at the right time to avoid any delays to the examination of your thesis. Institutions may require the forms to be presented some time before your thesis in order to enable them to find an appropriate external examiner.

Informing your departments of problems

If you feel there are any matters which have adversely affected the preparation of your thesis, it is vital that these are drawn to the attention of your supervisor or head of department at the earliest opportunity. You will need to provide any medical notes that back up such matters when you submit your thesis. If you have had problems with your supervision, this must have been drawn to the attention of your head of department before submission if it is to be considered as a mitigating factor.

In many institutions, candidates are allowed to suspend their studies if exceptional circumstances, e.g. ill health, severe financial hardship, arise. In these cases the submission date would be put back by the time period of the suspension, usually up to a maximum of a year. In most other cases you will be expected to submit on time and your thesis will not be considered if you do not meet the deadline.

Assessing the thesis

Now you have finally handed in your thesis you can sit back and relax for a bit. There is nothing you can actively do at this stage, but you will probably find it helpful to have some idea of what is happening to your work and when you can expect to hear whether you have been successful or not. If you expect to have an oral examination (viva), you can go over your thesis, looking for alterations you might like to make – this will be helpful preparation.

Explaining the examination procedures

Each university will have a clearly laid down examination procedure for each course that it runs which should be set out in your course handbook. The procedure at your university will involve one of:

▶ internal examination only
▶ external examination only
▶ both internal and external examination.

A viva may be involved in any of these three possible procedures.

Internal examination only

The role of the internal examiner is to decide whether your work and knowledge meet the standard which would normally be expected of a student in your department who was submitting for the same degree and meets the university's criteria for the award of the degree.

This is common and can take a number of forms:

1. Your supervisor alone will determine your mark.

2. Another member (or members) of your department or institution who has (have) not been involved in your supervision will mark your work.

3. Your supervisor and another member of your department and institution will both read your thesis and agree a mark between them.

The marks from any of these three possibilities may be subject to approval by an examination board.

External examination only
An appropriate person, with experience in the field from outside the institution will have been selected as your external examiner (your supervisor may well act as external examiner for a course in another institution). External examiners are usually paid a small sum for this service and are given a clear deadline for return of the thesis and usually a copy of the university regulations so they know whether the thesis you have presented is not only sound from a subject point of view but that it meets the word limits and formatting criteria.

The external examiner will normally only have your thesis on which to base the mark, will not have discussed it with your supervisor and will judge it on its own merits. The role of the examiner is to determine whether your thesis meets the appropriate academic standards and that you have achieved a standard comparable to that of a student being examined for the same degree in the same academic discipline in another university.

Internal and external examination
Two examiners will assess your work, one from inside your institution and one from outside. The two examiners will look at your thesis independently and reach a joint result. If, as rarely happens, this is not possible then it is usual for a second external examiner to be elected to consider your research. The examiners usually have equal status in examining you and your work – however, on a difficult academic issue, more weight may be placed on the advice of the external examiner, as they can offer a more independent view of your case.

Post-assessment issues

When you receive your results, hopefully you will be in a position to celebrate. You might want to consider publishing your work or going on to do further research such as a doctorate.

However, many candidates are not in this position immediately. You will usually receive one of the following results, although you should bear in mind that, in some institutions, the process can be more straightforward or more complex.

You have passed
It is usual at Master's level to obtain a straight pass, although increasingly universities are introducing some gradation of result, for example, distinction, merit, pass. You would normally have to achieve exceptionally high marks, often in both the taught examinations and the thesis to obtain a distinction (usually over 70%).

Minor amendments
This is still a very encouraging result. You will be given clear instructions about what amendments need to be undertaken and a short deadline in which to carry them out. These are usually typographical in nature.

Oral interview (viva)
The majority of institutions do not require Master's students to attend a viva. However, some do viva borderline candidates, or even a majority of candidates. You will not know why you have been asked to attend a viva, but it is important that you understand that, should you be a borderline candidate, your percentage mark can only stay the same or improve as a result of the viva. You should be positive and be ready to explain where you think you could have done a better job in retrospect.

Resubmission
The examiners consider that your thesis is representative of original work and could be amended to obtain a Master's degree. Usually they will have identified some fundamental flaws in the research and you will be required to address these and resubmit within a given, longer, time period, usually between 6 and 12 months. A resubmission fee will usually be payable (usually between £50–£150). If you prefer you can decide not to resubmit and settle for a diploma instead.

Failure
The examiners have determined that the thesis does not meet the academic standards for the Master's course and that they cannot award the degree. In most cases, provided your taught course examination results were satisfactory you would still be eligible for the diploma. You have the right of appeal against such a decision.

Appealing against your examination result
If you feel that your examination was not fair or that extenuating circumstances have not been considered, you can appeal against the result. Unless your appeal is related to the quality of your supervision, your supervisor is probably the best person to help and advise you at this time and ensure that your appeal is realistic.

Most universities have well established appeals procedures which will either be in your departmental handbook or available from your departmental office or university central administration. Get a copy of the regulations and see whether you would be able to appeal.

Determining your right to appeal

An appeal would usually be considered in the following circumstances.

▶ Where you could show that the examination procedure was not carried out appropriately and that this is likely to have affected the examiners' judgement, for example, your thesis was sent to an inappropriate external examiner or was delayed in some way.

▶ That there were exceptional circumstances, such as ill health, bereavement or poor supervision which affected your thesis and of which the examiners were not aware. You should have informed your examination convenor of this at the time that you submitted, but if you did and the information was not considered, or if you can show good reasons why the information was not provided, you would have grounds for appeal.

▶ That one or more of the examiners did not carry out an adequate assessment or was biased or prejudiced for some reason. This one is very hard to prove.

Appeals should not be entered into lightly as they will take a lot of time and energy on your part and that of your supervisor. Ensure that you are being realistic about whether your failure really was unreasonable.

In many cases you will have to act quickly and make an appeal within a short time, occasionally as little as a week, although most places allow at least a month. Appeals are considered at a very senior level, often by the vice-chancellor, before being referred to a committee for consideration. This can take some time and you may be called on to provide further evidence to support your appeal and will often have the opportunity to attend an appeal hearing.

Receiving the results of your appeal

The outcome of your appeal will be sent to you formally in writing and will usually be one of three things:

▶ Rejection of the appeal, a decision you would have to accept.

▶ Resubmission of the thesis for re-examination in its present form but ensuring that the examiners are now aware of the extenuating circumstances of which they were not informed before. In most cases, new examiners would be appointed and they may or may not be aware that they are undertaking a re-examination. It is usual in these cases for both the original and the new examiners' reports then to be considered by the Examination Board.

▶ Permission for you to revise the thesis and resubmit it for examination (usually where you received incorrect administrative advice on presentation or where a complaint about poor supervision was upheld).

Case studies

Russell burns the midnight oil

Russell has progressed erratically during the writing-up period – either producing large volumes of work between meetings with his supervisor, or avoiding the meetings so he does not to have to face up to his lack of progress for a few weeks. The submission deadline is marked clearly on his calendar and he has a pile of notes from his supervisor urgently requesting a meeting to look at the final draft. Russell looks at them all woefully as he finalises next season's rugby schedule on his computer.

Eventually, two weeks before the deadline, his supervisor corners him in the coffee shop and drags Russell back to fetch his disks. The supervisor is surprised that the final draft is nearly finished and that the quality of the work is better than might have been expected. However, Russell has thrust the departmental handbook underneath the leg of his desk to stop it wobbling, and has not consulted the regulations on format and presentation. His supervisor helpfully draws Russell's attentions to the relevant sections and draws up an action plan to enable him to meet the submission deadline.

Russell spends most of the next fortnight at his computer day and night, finalising his content and reformatting the part he had already completed. The rugby schedule is thrust under the leg of the desk in place of the handbook and his mates are amazed when he does not turn up for training.

Russell hands his thesis in the day before the deadline. The examiners agree that the thesis is academically sound and it is referred back to him for minor amendments only, although the examiners do note that the use of a spell checker would have been beneficial.

David goes his own way

David presents his final draft of the thesis to his supervisor a month before the deadline. He has typed it himself and paid meticulous attention to the university regulations regarding presentation. However, despite the numerous occasions that his supervisor has tried to redirect his thinking and helped him to restructure the thesis and consider new material, David has decided to stick to his original plan.

The supervisor once again makes a number of suggestions but at this stage, even if David were prepared to consider changes, they would be too monumental to make in time. David goes away, makes a few minor corrections to appease his supervisor, and hands the thesis in well in advance of the deadline.

Both the external and internal examiner are agreed that the thesis does not represent the standard of work required and that there are basic flaws in the research. David is invited to undertake major amendments and resubmit his thesis within a year.

Catherine gets nervous

One month before the deadline for submission, Catherine rather nervously takes her final draft along to her supervisor. She leaves the dissertation with him and goes back and tries very unsuccessfully not to think about whether he is at that minute reading it and what he thinks about it.

At the end of the week, she even more nervously knocks on his door and is invited in. The supervisor has been through the thesis in detail and makes a few suggestions concerning improvements in style and things that could be added or omitted. Catherine is rather embarrassed that the supervisor is so glowing in his praise of the final draft and goes back to do the amendments with renewed vigour.

Catherine's thesis is submitted one week before the deadline and she decides to go to stay with friends for a week or so to recover from the hard work and stress. Soon after she returns, the result comes through to say that she has passed. Her supervisor says that she narrowly missed obtaining a distinction and he strongly urges her to consider further research in the field.

Discussion points

1. What actions do you think you could take before beginning your writing up, to save you time and help you to comply with your university regulations and submit in the right format on time?

2. Do you know what happens at your university after you have submitted your thesis? How long do you have to wait for a result, how are you informed?

3. What happens at your university if you do not pass straight away? What right of appeal do you have? Do you think the procedure seems fair?

Questions and answers

Q. *I have not been given any written information regarding the submission of my thesis. I am about to begin writing up and need to know what is required. My supervisor is very vague about the regulations. Who should I approach?*

A. Now is definitely the time to get this information. Go to your department or faculty office first of all and see if they have some documentation. Failing that, maybe your university has a graduate school? If you have no luck with any of these you will have to venture into your university administration and get a copy of the university regulations and examine these in detail. If your university does not provide helpful documentation, report this to your student representative. If people do not complain, things may never get better.

Q. *I have not been happy with my supervision and this has made work on my dissertation much more difficult than for others on the course. I feel that this may have adversely affected my thesis. What can I do?*

A. Your university should have an established procedure for dealing with this and it is important that you find out about this straight away. Ask in your departmental office or make an appointment to see your head of department. Steps you might take are listed below:

▶ speak informally about your concerns to your supervisor

▶ make an appointment to see your head of department (if the supervisor is the problem a new one could be found at this stage)

▶ a formal procedure can be instigated which would usually involve you making a written complaint

▶ your complaint may be considered by the examiners when your thesis is examined. Do not leave making a complaint until you receive the results of your thesis.

Q. *I have been invited to attend a viva examination. I want to know why I have been singled out and what I can expect.*

A. There is no need to worry about an oral examination. Your supervisor may be able to explain to you why you have been selected. It could be for one of a number of reasons, such as:

▶ the examiners are required to viva candidates from the course and you were chosen at random

▶ your result is borderline in some way (it could be close to a distinction for example)

▶ the mark you received was equal to the average for your course and therefore you make a good marker for the external examiner to refer to when carrying out vivas for borderline cases in your group.

An oral examination is nothing to worry about but naturally you should prepare thoroughly for it. Reread your thesis and ensure you are up to date on any recent developments in the field. The purpose of the examination will be to test your general knowledge of the field and to question you on matters of detail arising from your thesis. It is an opportunity for you to discuss your work with two specialists in the field – make the most of it!

8

Explaining How to Publish
Alan Bond

One-minute summary – Publishing makes your research more accessible than if it were constrained to two copies of a thesis based at the institution where it was written. At the same time it will give you an advantage over your peers who have also gained a Master's-level degree. This chapter will explain how to go about publishing your research and will be structured under the following headings:

▶ deciding whether you want to publish
▶ deciding where you want to publish
▶ understanding the supervisor's role in publishing
▶ understanding the publishing process.

Deciding whether you want to publish

You're either about to finish or have finished your Master's thesis, so why would you want to think about publishing?

It is worth pointing out that, if you are keen to get your name into print for whatever reason, the sooner you get things in motion the better. Why? Because research is not novel for long, if you don't publish your discoveries, someone else somewhere in the world will make the same discovery – albeit after you, but they'll get all the credit. A more practical reason is that your research will still be fresh in your mind and you'll find it easier to change the format of your work to suit that required by the publishers you have chosen, and to respond to the comments of reviewers where appropriate.

Possible reasons why you might want to publish
A number of possible, equally valid, reasons why you might wish to publish your research work are listed below.

▶ You fancy a career as an academic.
▶ You feel that your research is important and that other people should have easy access to it.
▶ You feel that publishing is the obvious next step after your Master's.
▶ You want to get your name known.
▶ You simply want to see if you can.

► It will help your CV as it will demonstrate the value of your research and that you are capable of being pro-active and getting more from your Master's than the average student.

► The reason may be a combination of these.

Deciding where you want to publish

Before you can decide where to publish, you need to have worked out the reasons for publishing.

The number of journals being published has increased over the years and, from the point of view of publishing, this has good and bad points. Taking the good points first, there is more likely to be a journal publishing in your own field of research which should make it much easier to place your article and should mean that it is easier for you to find a journal which is directly related to your field of study. On the down side, it means you will have to look through a lot of journals to make sure you have found the most appropriate one.

What are the possibilities?
The types of publications for which you may like to aim can be divided into three:

1. **Peer review journal**. This is a journal published periodically which will ask a number of referees (normally two) to review articles submitted for publication to check whether the research is suitable material. A peer review journal will normally have a limited distribution to a number of libraries, academics and companies who subscribe. The length of articles varies, but they are typically about 5,000 words.

2. **Journal/magazine with no peer review**. These tend to be published more frequently than peer review journals and usually have a much larger circulation (in the thousands). Articles from such publications do get referenced by other workers. The length of articles varies, but are typically around 2,000 words.

3. **Book or book chapter**. The advice at this point would be not to run before you can walk! Most book publishers would prefer you to have some experience of publishing journal articles before you take on a book.

What is appropriate?
Table 11 will help to narrow down the sort of journal you should be looking for based on the possible reasons for publishing combined with the possible outlets listed above.

Table 11 Choosing where to publish

Possible reasons why you might want to publish	What are the possibilities?
You might fancy a career as an academic.	You should be aiming for a peer review journal as publication in these is necessary for a successful research career within the academic world.
You might feel that your research is important and that other people should have easy access to it.	Research which is published in a peer review journal is taken more seriously by colleagues than non-refereed work. At the same time, publication in a more popular publication reaches a wider audience.
You feel that publishing is the obvious next step after your Master's.	For an academic, this is true. If this is the career you intend to pursue, then go for a peer review journal, if not, then try to think of why it is an obvious step for you and then refer to this table again.
You want to get your name known.	Any sort of publication will get your name known, but you should think about the reasons why you want to get your name known to narrow it down more. One possibility is to publish both in a peer review journal and in a non-peer reviewed journal.
You simply want to see if you can.	It is harder to publish in a peer review journal – how much of a challenge do you want?
It will help your CV as it will demonstrate the value of your research and that you are capable of being proactive and getting more from your Master's than the average student.	Your CV will be helped by any sort of publication, but to get the most out of your CV, you should think about how you are going to use it and where you will send it – then look at the appropriate category in this table.
The reason may be a combination of these.	You probably want to publish in both types of outlet.

A common approach these days is to submit an article for a peer review journal and a shorter article for a magazine with a wider circulation. This way, the research is reported and checked by your peers, and your name is recognised by a wider audience. It should be stressed at this point, that once a magazine/journal has accepted your paper, you cannot submit the same article elsewhere. For this reason, care has to be taken in writing more than one article from the same piece of research.

Understanding the supervisor's role in publishing

Assuming that you have never published before, your supervisor can help you a lot and may be able to:

▶ give useful advice
▶ edit draft copies for you
▶ co-write the paper.

Don't be afraid of suggesting the latter option, your supervisor's career depends on publishing papers and, time permitting, they may be very pleased indeed to get involved. If this does happen, you should still be the first-named author on the submitted paper because it was your research, and work at this stage by the supervisor is not likely to be anywhere near the time you spent on the original research.

On behalf of supervisors, I would also recommend that you do acknowledge the time they've put into helping you in your work. If their input has really helped to shape the research or paper, then they do deserve to be a co-author. If they have simply been able to offer good advice at the right time without becoming heavily involved, an acknowledgement in the paper itself would not go amiss.

Understanding the publishing process

The following list will take you through a series of steps which you should follow in order to identify a suitable journal for publishing and to put the article in the appropriate format. You can also follow the steps through the flow diagram shown in Figure 23.

Make sure that the journal is interested in what you have to offer
Contact the editor by email, fax, letter or phone. The editor is likely to be an academic for whom the journal is only part of his/her work. They will also have lecturing and research responsibilities. As such, they tend to be very approachable and, if they do feel your potential article is unsuited to their journal, they may well have good suggestions for more suitable outlets.

Copy the 'notes for authors'

Most journals have a section entitled 'notes for authors' in each issue; sometimes they aren't to be found in the journal itself but can be obtained from the editor, publishers or, more commonly these days, a journal web page. For example, notes for authors can be found on the web pages of the

Journal of Environmental Planning and Management:
http://www.tandf.co.uk/journals/carfax/09640568.html
and the Journal of Environmental Management:
http://www.elsevier.com/locate/issn/0301-4797

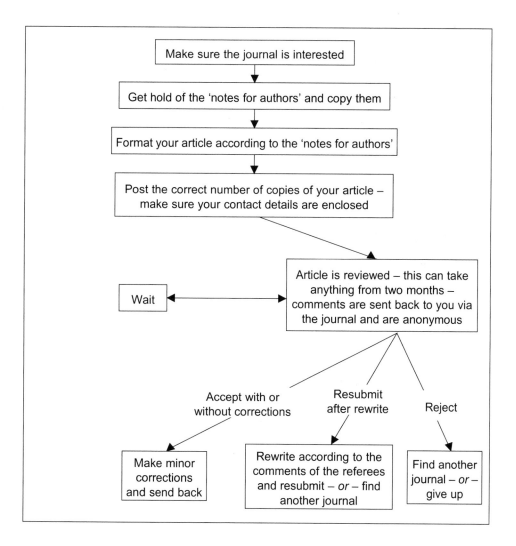

Figure 23. The publishing process.

Photocopy the 'notes for authors' and follow them when preparing your article. You will probably find that the article is required to be double spaced, single sided and that several copies are required, sometimes with additional copies of the summary on its own. If separate summaries are required, these will be so that the journal can send them to potential reviewers to ask them if they can and are interested in reviewing your article. Now you should see the reason for having contacted the journal earlier to see if they were interested in publishing. If you start at this stage, and format your article accordingly and make all the copies, then find out the subject areas don't match, it's a lot of wasted time and money.

Format your article according to the 'notes for authors'
Don't underestimate the amount of time this may take – a diagram or table you spent days preparing may need redrawing if you are required to change the line spacing within it! If you continue to write articles in the future, this problem will occur less frequently as you will begin to prepare all your diagrams and tables in a more appropriate format for publishing.

Send your article to the address specified in the notes for authors
Make sure that you have enclosed the correct number of copies of everything you were asked for. This may have included a floppy disk of your work. Don't forget to enclose a covering letter with your contact details!

Wait!
After you have submitted, you can do nothing but wait while the following stages are being worked through:

▶ the journal will be checking that the article is within their remit
▶ the journal will be finding referees
▶ the referees will be reviewing the article
▶ the journal will post or email back the reviews to you.

What happens in each of the stages will now be discussed in more detail.

The journal is checking that the article is within their remit
What will happen after the journal receives your proposed article is that they will check that the subject matter is appropriate. If something goes wrong at this stage, and the editor feels that the article is inappropriate and sends it back – this does not mean it isn't publishable. It means that the editor felt that the subject of the article did not fit within the remit of the journal and so did not consider it. You should approach a different journal instead.

The journal is finding referees
What is more likely to happen is that two copies of the article (which you will probably have supplied yourself) will be sent to two different referees with

expertise in the subject area covered by the article. You should realise that there are a lot of journals and a limited number of experts – to be eligible to review a journal article simply requires that a person has published in the field themselves, hence the journal will be aware of their existence.

The referees review your article

The two reviewers will receive your article with some instructions sent by the journal for reviewing it. Typically these will include:

▶ a (proposed) deadline for review, commonly about four weeks;

▶ criteria for evaluation; for example the quality and content of the research, quality brevity and clarity of presentation, and significance, relevance and timeliness of the topic; and

▶ a list of recommendations for the reviewer to choose from – such as:
  – acceptance, with or without minor revisions;
  – acceptance, subject to more significant changes;
  – rejection, but for re-evaluation after major revisions; or
  – rejection.

The reviewers will complete a short report stating their recommendation and detailing how the article fares against the criteria. They will send this back to the journal.

The journal will post or email back the reviews to you

The journal will wait until they have both reviews before writing to you with copies of the reports – usually you will never know who reviewed your article.

It is not uncommon to wait six months – it will depend on how quickly the administration of the journal works and on when the referees find the time to review the article. Most reviewers are busy and often leave the review until the last minute! When you do get your reviewer comments back, you should bear in mind that, if asked to look over a piece of work – however good it is, you will always alter something! In fact, if your supervisor has read through any of your work more than once, you may have found that he/she altered something you had written on the first edit, and then changed it back to how it was on the second edit! I point this out because there are likely to be a number of issues highlighted by the reviewers which they feel need changing. You will also probably find that the reviewers don't agree with each other, which makes it very difficult for you to make sensible changes. It is not uncommon for one reviewer to accept an article and another to reject it.

Make changes

The reviews you receive will explain what work needs to be done in order to edit the article so that it can be published. Make the changes but do not compromise your beliefs in doing this – everyone is entitled to a view and you should only make changes where you agree with them. At the same time, don't be too protective of your work, the referees are experienced people and will have suggested changes for a good reason.

Case studies

Russell considers the merits of publication

Russell was happy to have been awarded an MA and began to become a little concerned about his future. He did not have a job lined up and hadn't really felt the need to think about it previously. Now he was faced with unemployment and he began to wonder whether publishing his Master's might give him an edge in the job market. At the same time, he had no desire to go anywhere near his research again, he felt it had been an enormous weight off his shoulders to have finished writing his thesis and submitting it. Why would he want to start again? He eventually decided that 'needs must' and went to see his supervisor who encouraged him strongly to try to publish and even offered to help edit the paper. They agreed a deadline for the first draft to be given to the supervisor by Russell. However, Russell found it hard to motivate himself to produce a draft – there always seemed to be something more interesting to do. After several months, his supervisor called him in to tell him that he had just been asked to referee a paper for a journal which superseded the research Russell had carried out – it was too late!

David tries to salvage his job prospects

Having been asked to resubmit his thesis, David was worried about the job offer being held for him by the firm he had worked for during his year in industry; he saw the idea of publishing as a way of proving to his potential employers that his research was indeed of good quality. With this in mind, he went to the library and picked out a very well known and respected international journal and looked through it to find if there were any details on submitting papers; he couldn't see any so he took down the address of the editor. He then spent some weeks rewriting his thesis, bearing in mind the report he had received from the examiner who he felt had been pedantic. Having done this, he filed away his rewritten thesis because he wasn't permitted to resubmit until six months had gone by, and sent two copies of the same document to the editor of the journal. Judging by what he'd heard about publishing, he expected to hear from the referees at about the same time that he resubmitted his thesis. He was a little shocked to find his paper sent back to him after two weeks with a polite letter explaining that the journal did not have time to consider articles submitted in an inappropriate format, and that it was approximately four times too long anyway.

Catherine grows in confidence

Having successfully obtained her Master's, Catherine really started to believe in her own abilities. She was excited about the prospect of publishing her work and, after talking to her supervisor, was flattered that it was indeed suitable material. She spent a day in the library looking through law journals and making notes about the type of article they published and then annotating the 'notes for authors' which she found. She then arranged a meeting with her supervisor and talked about publishing an article. They agreed to work together with Catherine as the first author. They organised the structure and Catherine edited her thesis down to 5,000 words and gave it to her supervisor; after more editing and another meeting, the paper was submitted to what they both agreed was a suitable journal. The paper was accepted four months later by both referees with only minor editing needed.

Discussion points

1. What do you think you would get out of publishing your research?

2. Do you know of a journal which is exactly right for the research area you are interested in? If so, what is its title?

3. How important do you think it is to get the format of your article exactly as the publisher wants it? What will happen if you don't?

Questions and answers

Q. *My supervisor doesn't think that there is sufficient novel material in my thesis to warrant its publication in a peer review journal, but I really want to carry on in academia and I need to start publishing for my career. What should I do?*

A. At this stage you should try to get a second opinion from another member of staff. Your best approach is not to do this behind your supervisor's back, but tell him/her about your worries and why you want to publish and ask for help; ask if they feel that it is a good idea to ask someone else.

Q. *I've had comments back from two referees on my article, one of them felt that it was OK and just needed a few small problems sorting out, the other thought that the research area was not within the remit of the journal and for that reason should be rejected. What do I do?*

A. Look on the bright side, neither referee has said your research isn't up to scratch! The best thing to do is to talk to your supervisor about what has happened. It is often possible simply to make some changes which alter the emphasis of your article so that it does fit within the remit of the journal – this does not change your research or mean you have to do more research. It usually won't mean that you need to find another journal, although the final decision will be at the discretion of the editor.

Q. *My supervisor is pushing me to publish the research, but I've just started a job in an unrelated field and I'm really short of time. I can't see any value for my career in publishing. What do I say to my supervisor?*

A. One possibility is to suggest that the supervisor prepare a paper for publication. Explain that you are too busy at present, but would be happy to co-author a paper if the supervisor is prepared to find the appropriate journal and carry out all the required editing. You will need to discuss who should be the first-named author as this is quite important for prestige – it really should be you because it is your research and the supervisor is not likely to spend anything like the amount of time in editing your work that you put into the research. If more research is required this may change.

Glossary

Attitudinal data An attitude is the tendency to evaluate something in a particular way. Attitudinal data present measures of such evaluations, and can come in several different forms – rated numerically, or along various scales.

Bibliography The complete list of full publication details appended to a thesis. Not all of these may be cited in the text.

BIDS/ISI, Web of Knowledge OCLC FirstSearch Databases of journal articles available through the Internet. Full text can be downloaded.

Bookmark An Internet facility which helps you to find the same page again quickly.

Citation Bibliographic material acknowledging the work of another person. In the Harvard System, the author's name and the date of publication are inserted in brackets at the point in the text where the quotation occurs.

Code of practice Institutional statement of the standards and procedures expected or required of both students, and of supervisors and departments.

Confidential communication A communication between parties who stand in a confidential relationship with each other, and which the law protects.

Draft A version of the written-up account of research (either in full or part of it); usually a first or earlier version, as distinct from a 'final draft'.

Edit Careful perusal of your draft text to be sure that it makes sense and is consistent. Changes should be made to improve the precision and readability.

Empiricism An approach that stresses experience and observation to support knowledge claims.

Epistemology The grounds for knowledge claims.

Extensive research Research which looks for regularities and patterns amongst a broad population.

Focus group Unstructured interviews undertaken with small groups of people, making use of group dynamics to stimulate discussion. They are carried out not only to ascertain the group's views, but also to examine the dynamics within the group.

Generic skills Skills expected or required generally at a certain level of activity, as distinct from more specialised skills appropriate for a narrower area of activity. In the context of research, for instance, design and planning skills, communication and writing skills, and information technology skills would usually be classed as generic, as being necessary for any kind of research activity.

Headed paper Paper which contains the official logo or address of an institution or an organisation. It can be obtained for your institution by your thesis supervisor and will help to give your research enquiries authority.

Inspiration Software which enables the user to create diagrams of ideas and concepts. Outlines of the mind map can also be derived by the software.

Intensive research Research which concentrates on a particular case, or on a small number of cases, and seeks to address why and how specific sets of events and processes occur.

Interpretative (also known as Hermeneutics) An approach to social science that stresses the symbolic and meaningful aspects of social behaviour.

Interview schedule A list of topics, or even complete questions, which can be used to guide the order and nature of questions in an interview.

JANET Joint Academic Network. Connection to other academic libraries is possible via the Internet through your own library catalogue.

Libertas One of the On-line Public Assess Systems (OPACS) used in academic libraries. It includes: the catalogue, your own use of the library, and access to JANET.

Literature A term often used to indicate the secondary written sources for a particular subject, usually located in a library and comprising descriptive, critical or analytical commentary and discussion, frequently in the format of monographs and journal articles.

Master's degree Generally, indicating the first level of postgraduate degree study. In the UK a Master's degree may be based on a taught programme of studies, or purely based on research. (In the latter case it is usually designated an MPhil degree.)

Method/methodology The way in which research is carried out and sources are used (for instance, while 'library-based' research will use material and data located in libraries, 'fieldwork' gathers information from the actual situation being discussed in the research, for example asking questions of the people whose situation or behaviour is being investigated).

Methodology The critical analysis of methods.

Mind Map A note-taking technique promoted by Tony Buzan. Diagramming is used to show relationships of concepts and their components.

Ontology An account of the phenomena under study and the relationships between these phenomena.

Paragraph A group of sentences which introduces an aspect of an idea/argument/procedure; defines, gives examples and develops the topic; then brings all to a conclusion. A link to the next aspect or topic may be included. Paragraphs may be up to 10 sentences or as few as 2 sentences. One sentence paragraphs are not very helpful.

Parallel construction Sentence construction which follows the same format for a series of aspects in order to display the equality of relationship they all bear to the subject of the sentence or its verb. Lists or bullet points all need to begin with the same form of word, i.e., nouns, gerunds, infinitives, active verbs.

Plagiarism Copying the words written by another person without acknowledgement. This practice is viewed with grave concern in the academic community.

Population This refers to the unit or elements being studied. It need not be 'the population' as traditionally understood in terms of individuals living within a particular area, but can refer to any collection of items under research – e.g. a group of hospitals, or a number of local authorities, or a collection of shops.

Positivism A philosophy of science and social science that stresses empirical support and the generation of general laws to explain phenomena.

Project A particular research activity or programme.

Proof-read Reading a draft which is ready for submission to catch and correct mechanical errors of spelling, punctuation and formatting.

Qualitative data Data that are non-numeric in form, usually focusing on people's beliefs, values and meanings.

Quantitative data Data that are numeric, and able to be counted and quantified.

Rationalism An approach to knowledge production using faculties of reasoning.

Reference References are the full list of actual texts cited. Full publication details must be included.

Register The level of language represented by the preciseness of the vocabulary. Spoken registers are informal, including slang, conversational, colloquial and dialectal English; written registers are formal, including academic, professional and specialist language.

Regulations Precisely drafted and formal requirements relating to the programme of studies and process of assessment used for the award of a degree.

Relata In a proposition a term that is related to the proposition's referent.

Respondents Those who are the sources of your research information. They provide the data which you analyse and interpret.

Sampling The method through which an entire 'population' is reduced in size to manageable research proportions.

Sampling frame The list of population members from which the sample is drawn. Ideally it should contain a complete listing of every element in the target population.

Submission Handing over finally a completed piece of work (for instance, the thesis) for purposes of examination for the award of the degree.

Subordination A way of showing that information is less important than the main idea, but is, nevertheless, related to or has some effect on the main idea. A subordinated idea occurs in a clause which begins with words like, since, when, because, until, which, that...

Supervisor A member of the academic staff in a university or other higher education institution assigned to advise and monitor the progress of a student carrying out research for a degree.

Theory A logically interrelated set of abstractions, ideas and propositions about empirical reality that organises knowledge about the world.

Thesis A written account of research submitted for the award of a postgraduate degree. (Also used in a wider sense to refer to an argument or theory put forward in an academic context.)

Thesis statement A clear statement of the scope and parameters of your investigation; what factors limit those parameters; how the thesis is organised; and what methods will be employed to reach a conclusion.

Transition words Words which link one part of a sentence to another, one sentence to another, or paragraphs to each other. Included in this type are words like hence, therefore, moreover, nevertheless.

Transcript The word-by-word 'translation' of an interview from the tape recorder onto the written page, usually typed to facilitate further analysis.

Triangulation The use of multiple research methods and sources of data to 'check' individual accounts and build up a body of evidence.

Web search engine Search and index services which are useful paths to finding information more easily on the Internet are: AltaVista; Goggle; Infoseek; Lycos; Yahoo!.

Widows and orphans A term used to identify parts of the word processed text. If one line of a list (or a title of a section) is left at the bottom of a page, it is called a *widow*. If one line of a list is left at the top of a page, it is called an *orphan*.

Bibliography

Chapter 2

Chalmers, A. F. (1992) *What is This Thing called Science?* Buckingham, Open University Press.
Delanty, G. (1997) *Social Science: Beyond Constructivism and Realism.* Buckingham, Open University Press.
Hammersley, M. (1997) *Social Research: Philosophy, Politics and Practice.* London, Sage.
Harré, R. (1970) *The Principles of Scientific Thinking.* London, Macmillan.
Kuhn, T. (1970) *The Structure of Scientific Revolutions.* Chicago, University of Chicago Press.
May, T. (1996) *Situating Social Theory.* Buckingham, Open University Press.
Popper, K. (1959) *The Logic of Scientific Discovery.* London, Hutchinson.
Sayer, A. (1992) *Method in Social Science: A Realist Approach.* London, Routledge.
Smith, M. J. (1998) *Social Science in Question,* London, Sage.

Chapter 3

Since we have covered an immense range of issues in a very short time, the following list contains all the references used in Chapter 3 but also gives the details of a variety of other books on qualitative data. Some concentrate on particular methods or specific forms of data, others are more general.

Chapter references

Cloke, P., Crang, P., Goodwin, M., Painter, J. and Philo, C. (2002) *Practising Human Geography: The Construction and Interpretation of Geographical Data.* Sage.
Davis, M. (1990) *The City of Quartz.* Verso.
Dey, I. (1993) *Qualitative Data Analysis: A User Friendly Guide for Social Scientists.* Routledge.
Hammersley, M. & Atkinson, P. (1984) *Ethnography: Principles in Practice.* Routledge.
Kitchin, R. and Tate, N. (2000) *Conducting Research into Human Geography.* Prentice Hall.
Sayer, A. (1992) *Method in Social Science: A Realist Approach.* Routledge.
Scott, J. (1990) *A Matter of Record: Documentary Sources in Social Research.* Polity Press.

Thomas, W. I. and Znaniecki, F. (1927) *The Polish Peasant in Europe and America* (2d edn). New York: Dover (2 volumes).
Walcott, H. (1995) *The Art of Fieldwork*. AltaMira Press.

Additional helpful material
Berg, B. (1989) *Qualitative Research Methods for the Social Sciences*. Allyn and Bacon.
Burgess, R. (1984) *In the Field*. Allen and Unwin.
Frankfort-Nachmias, C. and Nachmias, D. (1996) *Research Methods in the Social Sciences*. Edward Arnold.
Mason, J. (1996) *Qualitative Researching*. Sage.
Rose, D. (1990) *Living the Ethnographic Life*. Sage.
Silverman, D. (1993) *Interpreting Qualitative Data: Methods for Analysing Talk, Text and Interaction*. Sage.
Strauss, A. (1987) *Qualitative Analysis for Social Scientists*. Cambridge University Press.

Chapter 4

Campbell, N. (1952) *What is Science?* Dover Publications.
Cohen, J. and Chen, P. (1983) *Applied Multiple Regression/Correlation Analysis for the Behavioral Sciences*. Hillsdale, New Jersey: Lawrence Erlbaum Associates.
Conover, W. (1980) *Practical Nonparametric Statistics*. New York: John Wiley & Sons, Inc.
Giles, J. (1972) *Real Analysis*. Sydney: John Wiley & Sons Australasia Pty Limited.
Shock, N. (1951) 'Growth Curves', in S. Stevens (ed.), *Handbook of Experimental Psychology*. New York: John Wiley & Sons, Inc., pp. 330–346.
Siegel, S. and Castellan, N. (1988) *Non Parametric Statistics for the Behavioral Sciences*. New York: McGraw-Hill Book Company.
Stevens, S. (1946) 'On the Theory of the Scales of Measurement', *Science*, CIII (7 June, 1946), pp. 677–680.
Stevens, S. (1951) *Handbook of Experimental Phsychology*. New York: John Wiley & Sons, Inc.
Stevens, S. (1955) 'On the Averaging of Data', *Science*, CXXI (28 January 1955), pp. 113–116.
Stevens, S. (1968) 'Measurement, Statistics and the Schemapiric View', *Science*, CLXI (30 August, 1968), pp. 849–856.
Torgerson, W. (1958) *Theory and Methods of Scaling*. New York: John Wiley & Sons, Inc.

Chapter 5

Achtert, W.S. (1985) *The MLA Style Manual*. MLA.

British Standards Institution (1990) *Recommendations for Citing and Referencing Published Material* (2nd edn). British Standards Institution.

Buzan, T. (1988) *Make the Most of Your Mind*. Pan Books.

Eastwood, J. (1994) *Oxford Guide to English Grammar*. Oxford University Press.

Hall, C. (1994) *Getting Down to Writing: A Student's Guide to Overcoming Writer's Block*. Peter Francis Publishers.

Iansyst Training Products (undated) Inspiration software, Professional Edition for Higher Education. The White House, 72 Fen Road, Cambridge, CB4 1UN. Freephone 0500 141515.

Spink, J. (1982) *A Manual for Writers of Research Papers, Theses and Dissertations*. 1st British Edition. Heinemann.

American Edition: Turabian, K.L. (1973) *A Manual for Writers of Term Papers, Theses and Dissertations*. Chicago University Press.

Chapter 6

Darley, B., Griew, A., McLoughlin, K. and Williams, J. (1994) *How to Keep a Clinical Confidence*. HMSO.

Farrington, D. (1998) *The Law of Higher Education* (2nd edn). Butterworths, pp. 512–13.

Flint, M.F., Fitzpatrick, N. and Thorne, C. (2000) *A User's Guide to Copyright* (4th edn) Butterworths.

Garnet, K., Rayner James, J. and Davies, G. (1999) *Copinger and Skone James on Copyright* (14th edn). Sweet and Maxwell.

Kennedy, I. and Grubb, A. (2000) *Medical Law* (3rd edn). Butterworths. Chapter 8.

Laddie, H., Prescott, I. and Vittoria, M. (2000) *The Modern Law of Copyright* (3rd edn). Butterworths.

Padfield, T. (2001) *Copyright for Archivists and Users of Archives*. Public Record Office.

Index